PRAISE FOR ALEXIS ABRAMSON AND
The Caregiver's Survival Handbook

"You can trust Alexis Abramson to help you through the emotional and physical demands of caring for your aging parents. Alexis is driven by a sincere desire to *help* people *help* the people they love."
   —Ann Curry, NBC's *Today* show

"The world is aging and we are all becoming aware of increased longevity. What we do not recognize is how each of us will inevitably face the great equalizer—*caregiving*. Alexis Abramson makes a significant contribution to this demographic reality by providing us an invaluable roadmap for how we care for others as they age and how we want to be cared for. Among the many insights she offers is another demographic truism: that aging and caregiving is heavily about women; their longer life expectancy and the inordinate responsibility they face as caregivers. This book is a *must read* for all of us!"
   —Dr. Fernando M. Torres-Gil
      Former U.S. Assistant Secretary on Aging
      U.S. Department of Health and Human Services
      Director, UCLA Center for Policy Research on Aging

"Few entrepreneurs have focused more sharply on the needs of older Americans than Alexis Abramson."
   —*Time* magazine

"Abramson dreams of a "barrier-free society" for seniors and disabled people."
   —*Style* magazine

"In my 26 years of working for AARP, I have encountered few people who had the knowledge, experience and passion that Alexis possesses for serving older persons. Alexis has accomplished a lot and has gained a well-deserved national reputation as an authority on issues affecting older persons."
   —Horace B. Deets
      Former Executive Director, AARP

THE CAREGIVER'S SURVIVAL HANDBOOK

How to Care for Your Aging Parent without Losing Yourself

ALEXIS ABRAMSON

with *Mary Anne Dunkin*

A Perigee Book

A Perigee Book
Published by The Berkley Publishing Group
A division of Penguin Group (USA) Inc.
375 Hudson Street
New York, New York 10014

Perigee trade paperback edition: August 2004

Visit our website at www.penguin.com

Library of Congress Cataloging-in-Publication Data

Abramson, Alexis.
The caregiver's survival handbook : how to care for your aging parent without
losing yourself / Alexis Abramson with Mary Anne Dunkin.—1st Pedigree ed.
p.   cm.
"A Perigee book"
ISBN 0-399-52998-5
1. Aging parent—Care   2. Adult children of aging parents—Family
relationships.   3. Caregivers—Psychology.   I. Dunkin, Mary Anne.   II. Title.

HQ1063.6.A27 2004
646.7'8—dc22   2004044489

Printed in the United States of America

10 9 8 7 6 5 4

DEDICATION
I dedicate this book to my grandparents,
Mimi Rose, Popop Sam, Mimi Esther, and Popop Joe.

ACKNOWLEDGMENTS

I would like to thank *all* of my friends and family, especially the following individuals who graciously gave their time, effort and support during the writing of this book.

- To Sandra Craine who taught me what it means to be a strong leader.
- To Laura Rossman for her ongoing support and thoughtful advice.
- To Drs. Merril Silverstein and Fernando Torres-Gil for being my mentors and always providing me with enormous insight.
- To my sister-in-law Cara Abramson and friend Rana Walker for their enthusiasm and thoughtful comments on the manuscript.
- To Donald Minsk for his unwavering loyalty and continuous encouragement.
- To Susan Raihofer and everyone at the David Black Literary Agency, my agents and champions, without whom this book would have never come to fruition.
- To Michelle Howry, John Duff and everyone at Penguin and Perigee for their strong commitment to this project.
- To my Mom, who is both my role model and "(s)hero."
- To my Dad and Brother for their tremendous insight and unconditional love.
- To my nephews, Max and Micah Abramson, for always bringing out the child in me.
- To Louise Samsky, for her deep friendship and for always providing me with a wonderful respite for rest and recreation.
- To Mary Anne Duncan, for her dedication, commitment and passion to the writing of this book.

And finally, I wholeheartedly acknowledge all the caregivers who selflessly give their love, time and money to improve the quality of life for others.

CONTENTS

INTRODUCTION

On a brisk, late-autumn afternoon in 1996, I was working in Atlanta as the director of a senior adult center. Having completed my master's in gerontology, I was about to enter a doctoral program. Then something happened that changed my mind. I was walking down the main hall of the center and saw Peggy, one of the members under my care, sobbing, her arms draped over the hallway telephone. I gently inquired why she was upset, anticipating that she had received terrible news. But to my surprise, her tears were caused not by grief but by frustration: Peggy couldn't make out the numbers on the telephone keypad.

While dialing the number for her, I had what Oprah Winfrey calls a "lightbulb moment." I knew then that I wanted to do more than care for seniors; I realized that I also had to find ways to make their lives easier, more independent, and more fulfilling—and, by extension, simultaneously ease their caregivers' responsibilities. And it started with the simplest of things, like locating a keypad with larger push buttons that made it easier for Peggy and other residents with impaired vision to see the numbers to dial.

Within a week I found several items to make the center more "senior-friendly," including folding walking canes, telephone amplifiers, and large-number playing cards. The residents were thrilled, which in turn made me feel great. I deferred my doctorate scholarship and instead asked my parents for a loan to launch a retail clearinghouse for senior and caregiver products.

My first hire was my petite eighty-four-year-old grandmother, "Mimi" Rose, who is still going strong today at ninety-two years young. My grandmother has been a tremendous influence on my life, and in fact inspired me as a teenager to become a gerontologist. By embracing her senior years she has made them an exciting and challenging time, and I've made it my life's work to help other mature adults emulate the independent lifestyle that she has.

Eventually, my company became part of one of our distributors, and now I spend my time as an eldercare expert for many organizations and corporations such as AARP, Duracell, and Century 21. I also serve as a frequent gerontology guest expert on the NBC *Today* show, CNN, and many other national and international media outlets. It's my mission and my passion to get the word out about products, services, and coping strategies that can help seniors live more independent lives, which in turn frees up precious time for their overworked caregivers.

Before we go further, let me define what I mean by caregiver. Being a caregiver doesn't have to mean providing for your family member's *every* need—bathing, feeding, dressing, transporting, and so forth. But if you do those things, you certainly are a caregiver. If you run errands for an older parent, occasionally help with his housework or yard work, or balance his checkbook, you are also a caregiver. This book is for caregivers at both ends of the spectrum—and those in between.

Time and again I have found that even seemingly small changes in a family dynamic or society at large make a world of difference. As it stands now, caring for aging parents costs the average worker over her lifetime more than half a million dollars in lost wages. Clearly, caregivers need more paid leave, flextime, and onsite eldercare: It's good for employees *and* employers.

Mature adults need businesses to be more attuned to their needs as well. Easy-open aspirin bottles and levers rather than knobs on doors make life much easier for elders with arthritis. I've consulted with drugstore chains about the importance of stocking products for mature adults at eye level. After menopause, the average American woman loses an inch and a half in height each decade due to the collapse of the vertebrae in her spine, and putting items like incontinence products within her reach is crucial. What adult wouldn't feel embarrassed having to request help to reach for a box of Depends?

Sensitivity to the needs of elders is desperately lacking in this country. But the reality is that insensitivity toward both the elderly and caregivers is a virtual epidemic. Like women in other helping professions, caregivers are not shown the consideration they deserve. Caregivers, who give so much to others, are nevertheless often devalued and made to feel invisible. "It's as if," one caregiver told me, "we don't even exist."

As our society ages and the Baby Boomers reach the stage of life where our elderly parents are now, and I have no doubt that this segment of our population will become more visible and the treatment of its members will change for the better. This large and vocal generation, used to getting what it wants from life, will demand it. Nevertheless, long-held attitudes toward the elderly and their caregivers in our society may take many more years to change—unless we begin to empower our elders now. Doing so is not only our duty, it is our privilege, because by empowering our elders we empower ourselves.

That's why I decided to write *The Caregiver's Survival Handbook*. I wanted to validate and address the emotional and practical needs of caregivers, most of whom are women, and those they care for. Through *The Caregiver's Survival Handbook* I hope to empower caregivers to speak up, get help, and care for themselves *first* so that they can, in turn, care for others. I hope to give their concerns a voice—and with that voice, help restore the rights and dignity of our seniors and those who care for them.

One

HOW CAN I JUGGLE
MY VARIOUS
RESPONSIBILITIES?

66 "How can I juggle my various responibilities?" "Why do I feel so guilty?" "Will I ever get my life back?" These are some of the pressing questions I hear every day from over-worked caregivers who need help. For those in the sandwich generation—the majority of whom are women aged forty to sixty, caring for children and parents and often working outside the home—the biggest complaint is time . . . or lack thereof. This lack of time can lead to guilt, frustration, anger, fatigue, and eventually burnout. Caught between tending to parents and children, maintaining a home, and pursuing a career, many women admit to feeling overhelmed and *invisible*—taken for granted by their families and ignored by society.

One in four families in the United States is caring for parents or other mature relatives, and 72 percent of the primary care-givers in these families are women. Stated another way, of the 22 million "sandwiched" caregivers in this country, 16 million are women. You know who you are, and you know about the challenges you face—juggling a job and family responsibilities, making trips to the pediatrician as well as the geriatrician, caring for your parent without neglecting your husband or children, and making time for yourself when everyone else seems to want a piece of it. This book tackles your caregiver concerns by offering support and solutions to your seven most critical challenges.

When we feel pressure to be all things to all people, we tend to give one person the short end of the stick—ourselves. But playing the "martyr role" helps no one and is, in fact, a recipe for disaster. This book shows you how to find time for yourself by assertively soliciting the help of family members and professionals, encouraging parental self-sufficiency, and giving yourself permission to feel joy. You'll also learn how the pursuit of your own interests actually makes you a *better* caregiver.

If you talk with other women—even the seemingly perfect ones—who care for loved ones, you'll probably find they face many of the same challenges you do. Caregiving is *never* easy.

Whether we manage our loved ones' care from a rural trailer park or metropolitan high-rise, largely on our own or with an abundance of help, most of us do so with a great deal of love and compassion. Regardless of our circumstances, we are, in a sense, in this together. And we have a lot to learn from one another.

Caregivers often tell me that if they had more money, all of their caregiving problems would be solved. But while financial security usually brings a higher standard of care and helps ease stress, the *emotional* challenges of caring for a loved one occur regardless of financial circumstances.

When you think about it, it makes perfect sense. Surely you

want the best for your mom, but would all the money in the world bring back her youth and good health? Enough money can hire round-the-clock caregivers, but can it relieve the yearning to help your parents or ease the feelings that you should be doing it all yourself? Will a million dollars in your bank account or a condo in Maui make it any easier to accept that the person who once cared for you can no longer care for herself?

Caring for an ill or older parent obviously requires more than having enough money or enough help from family to provide the best care for them physically. It means giving of yourself—your time, your energy, and your love. The difficulty extends further than finding the money or other resources to keep going. It means seeing someone you love slowly—or perhaps quickly—slip away from you. No amount of money can make that easier to bear.

The emotional upheaval that comes with watching a loved one grow old and frail is only compounded by the other stresses we as women must face each day, regardless of our walk of life—rush-hour traffic; business meetings; job deadlines; demanding bosses, children, and spouses; dirty laundry, and unmade beds; family and community responsibilities; and insensitive family members and coworkers. Sometimes we feel like we're doing it all—with no recognition and no thanks from anyone. We give our attention to everything and everyone but ourselves. We feel invisible.

Do you feel overworked and underappreciated? You're not alone. Do you sometimes think you can't go on? Well, you can. Many people, like you, are caring for older parents while working hard to balance all of the other relationships and responsibilities in their lives. Countless others have gone before you and survived. You aren't alone. People who've been there and back offer the following survival tips for fellow caregivers.

Keep a Sense of Humor

Though caring for a loved one can quickly bring you down, do your best to guard against depression. Allowing yourself time to acknowledge your sadness is essential, and having a good cry now and then can be healing. But allowing yourself to get down in the dumps and stay there can be harmful to your emotional and physical health.

We've all heard that a merry heart is good medicine. But who can feel merry when caring for an ill and aging loved one? The answer is, *you* can. Find something that makes you laugh, even when you feel like crying. Get a *Far Side* calendar for your desk, rent some funny movies (or better yet, check them out of your local library for free), read the Sunday comics, or call an upbeat friend. Make a date with your spouse or a friend to see a favorite comedian. Look for humor in everyday situations.

"Sometimes the only way you can deal with life is to look at the funny side of it," says Gail Kort, fifty-seven, who, by many people's estimates, would have little reason to laugh. For most of her life she was a caregiver for *someone*—whether it be her mother, who developed rheumatoid arthritis as a young adult; her grandmother with Alzheimer's; or her father, who was disabled from a stroke—while coping with a chronic disease herself. Yet she still managed to find humor in some of the most difficult situations.

"When my father was in the nursing home, sometimes my sister and I would go see him and he didn't even know who we were," Kort recalls. "One day we went in and a young nurse was helping him. He introduced us to the nurse as his brother and his brother's wife. Some people would be very upset by that. But when my sister and I left, we were laughing. We asked each other, 'Which one of us was supposedly his brother?' "

If you think that by laughing you are making light of a serious situation, don't be so hard on yourself. Laughing is one of our most effective coping mechanisms, and can be one of your greatest allies against caregiver burnout. So look at the light side—or the *Far Side*—and have a good laugh.

Take Care of Yourself

If you're like most women, you somehow find the time to take care of the important people in your life, but in the process, you probably forget to take care of yourself. As we'll see in later chapters, taking care of yourself is essential if you want to be healthy enough to take care of others.

"Whatever you can do that's humanly possible to help [your parent], you must do," says actress Mariette Hartley, who cared for her mother with emphysema in the final months of her life. "But you must also take care of yourself . . . because once the person's gone, there's you. You have *your* life. If you don't have your life, what will you go back to?"

Taking care of yourself means eating right, getting adequate rest, and keeping up with your own medical appointments. But it also means allowing yourself some time to do the things you enjoy, even if they seem frivolous to those around you. Hartley advises spending a day at the spa or, if you can't afford that, having a friend give you a massage. "Buy some candles. Take a nice warm bath. Meditate," she recommends.

Taking care of yourself also means tending to your emotional needs, taking breaks from caregiving, and nurturing the other relationships in your life. "My life was filled . . . with my husband, with my children, with adopted children, with neighborhood children," says Hartley.

Even Gail Kort, whose life was filled with people who depended on her—her parents, her grandmother, her niece, and her nephew—found time to spend with one other very important person: a friend she's had since she was six years old. "Through the years, we've managed to get together at least once a month—even when I was caring for my parents and grandmother," says Kort. "I couldn't have gotten through this without my friends."

When you become a caregiver, someone is counting on you. The best way to ensure you don't let them—or yourself—down is to take care of yourself, so you can take better care of them.

Whether it's getting help from family, keeping up with your own medical appointments, or discovering activities you enjoy, the chapters ahead are filled with advice on how to take care of yourself. (For some tips on keeping up with friends while you're busy with caregiving, see "Maintaining Friendships" in Chapter 7.)

Take a Break

You deserve a break today. The words of this 1970s advertising slogan have a special meaning to a caregiver. If you care for an aging parent or parents—particularly if your parent lives in your home—you not only deserve a break, you *need* one.

Nobody understands this better than Beth Mallory. For the five years that her mother has lived with her, she has required constant care. Mallory, who is single and works an hour away from their home in Dublin, Georgia, hires sitters to stay with her mother while she's at work. But once home, she's it. "Mom's here seven days a week and I'm here seven days a week. She can't go anywhere, which means I can't go anywhere."

In her early days of caregiving, Mallory never left her mother unless she absolutely had to—for work or a quick trip to the grocery store or Wal-Mart. Some friends, however, encouraged her to take a break now and then. Mallory, desperate for some respite, listened. "Now, I hire a sitter sometimes just for a few hours so I can get out," she says. "Once a year I have someone watch my mother for a weekend so I can go to Atlanta and visit friends."

If taking a weekend or even a few hours isn't practical or even possible, take whatever you can get, advises Linda Dano, an actress on several daytime dramas and caregiver to her elderly mother with Alzheimer's disease. Ask friends or family members to help.

"If I could say one thing to caregivers, it would be that they must reach out for help, they must! They have to ask for help from family and friends, whether that be a simple, 'Please can you set the table because I've got to go to the bathroom, and I've got to put myself in a tub for ten minutes' or 'I need to walk around the block. I need to get out. I need a break,' " says Dano.

If a physical break or change of venue is beyond what you can manage, try taking a mental break now and then. Sneak in a chapter of a good book, watch an interesting TV show, or begin a craft project you can do while you are with your parent. "I think everybody needs a hobby, whether it's needlework, sewing, or stamp collecting," says Kort. "You need a break now and then to do what you enjoy."

As taxing as caregiving is, taking a breather whenever—and however—you can will help restore your energy, your focus, and your sanity to help you better cope with the task at hand. In Chapter 3, you'll learn how to get more help from those around you, and in Chapter 5 you'll find ways to help your parents do more for themselves, freeing up some time for you.

Be Grateful for the Time
You Have Together

No matter how long and hard caregiving may be, it won't go on forever. Cherish the fact that, for now, your loved one is still alive and with you.

Many successful caregivers have made it through difficult days by reminding themselves that life is precious and the opportunity to care for a parent in her final days, months, or years is a once-in-a-lifetime gift.

Actress Peri Gilpin cared for her mother, who was suffering from cancer, while starring in one of TV's hottest sitcoms, *Frazier*. Gilpin, known to *Frazier* fans as "Roz," was on hiatus from the show and visiting her family in Texas when her mother—who had been battling cancer for years—suffered a major setback with the disease. When Gilpin returned to the show, her mother, sister, and father followed her back to Los Angeles.

There, they all helped with her mother's care during the final months. Six months after arriving in L.A., Gilpin's mother died peacefully with her family surrounding her. "I'm so grateful for those six months. Mom and I got even closer," said Gilpin. "I had the honor of being there when she died. I think that was a gift."

Actress Mariette Hartley expresses similar sentiments over the final months she had with her mother. Although their relationship lacked affection and had been strained from Hartley's earliest memories, those last few months were a time of healing. "It was such a brilliant time for the two of us, because my mother allowed herself to be taken care of—really taken care of—for the first time in her life," Hartley said. "It was the first time that my mother and I held one another without one of us [instantly] letting go."

Though being a caregiver has been a huge commitment for her, Beth Mallory has cherished the five years she has cared for her mother. "We both have our days when we get on each other's nerves a little bit," says Mallory. "But for the most part she does really well to be her age and have the problems that she has. I wouldn't walk away [from caregiving] for anything. She's my mom and she's almost eighty-nine years old. Some people don't live to be eighty-nine years old. I'm just thankful to have her around."

If you find yourself as a caregiver for someone you love, consider that time of giving as something to be treasured for the rest of your life. Gilpin advises, "Although it seems impossible or that it can't be done, you can do it. With caregiving, you do not stop, but it is good. It is the best way to spend your time—to be able to do this for someone you love."

Ask Everyone to Pitch In

Just because you are caring for your parent, don't assume that she can't do things for herself—or for you. Everyone needs to feel useful and needed, and finding things your parent can do helps both of you.

"Identify things your loved ones can do and let them do those things," suggests Gail Kort. When caring for her mother and grandmother, Kort found ways that both of the women could be productive and feel useful. Because Kort's mother was not cognitively impaired, she was able to supervise the grandmother and direct her in doing household tasks, such as cooking. "Grandma could cook as long as my mother told her what to do and [subsequently] reminded her when it was time to take something out of the oven." What Kort's grandmother lacked in mental clarity, she made up for in physical strength and manual dexterity, which both Kort and her mother were without due to their debilitating arthritis. "When Grandma was so bad that she couldn't remember what she had for lunch ten minutes before, she was still able to stem green beans and help me open and close the pressure cooker. These were things she *could* do, and I always made sure that she still played an active part. She was involved in anything we were doing."

Before assigning tasks to your loved one, carefully consider what she is capable of. If she has trouble with standing or stamina, ask her to sort socks or fold laundry while sitting on the sofa or mix a cake batter while sitting at the kitchen table. You could also give her a high stool and have her dry and sort silverware at the kitchen sink. If arthritis in the joints of her hands makes tasks like these difficult, she might be able to do light housework, such as sweeping, dusting, or cleaning bathroom mirrors. (The new glass-cleaning wipes make this chore so much easier!) If you have children, ask if she will read to them, play card games with them, or just sit and tell them stories. The times spent with a grandparent are times every child remembers and cherishes.

Speaking of children, have them help out too. For a few years, in addition to caring for her older family members, Kort also took care of a young niece and nephew while their mother worked. While the children required some care, she said, they were also helpful. "They listened to Grandma's stories and entertained her. They kept her occupied, so I didn't have to worry about her walking out of the front door and into the street."

Managing a home while caring for an elderly family member can be a challenge, particularly if you have a family of your own. But many problems can be minimized—and morales boosted—by making those you care for part of the solution. In Chapter 5 you'll find some practical advice—not to mention a lot of helpful devices and gadgets—to help make your parent more independent and productive.

Don't Give in to Guilt

Though you may feel guilty when you can't do as much for your parent as you would like or think you should, don't give in to that guilt. "We can't let feelings of guilt overtake us," says Linda Dano, who watched her father slowly die in a nursing home from Alzheimer's disease prior to her mother's diagnosis with the disease.

"It was the most traumatic experience of my entire life, watching my dad every day get further and further away from us," remembers Dano. For Dano, the guilt of being unable to help her father was great. She dealt with her feelings of despair by eating and crying, but never spoke to anyone about his disease or even sought out information about it. "I thought, 'What's the point?' My father had already left me. I couldn't save him now."

Each time she visited her father in the nursing home, she would take the back stairs to leave the building. Why? Because before she left for home, she says, she would sit down and weep.

Even women who provide day-to-day, in-home care for an aging parent can feel guilt. They may feel guilty, if you can believe it, that they aren't doing enough for their parents or that they didn't spend more time with their parents before their health declined.

Despite the fact that she has spent most of her life caring for one or more family members, Gail Kort felt guilty going on with her own life after her elderly father went to live in a nursing home. "I thought I should not be out running around and having fun while my father was in the nursing home. I should be taking care of him, but I knew I couldn't do it and it was hard."

Other caregivers feel guilty for devoting too much time and attention to their parents because in doing so, they feel they are neglecting their jobs, their friends, and their other family members.

The bottom line is there are many reasons caregivers feel guilt. Most reasons for guilt are unwarranted and most effects of it are destructive. If you want to be an effective caregiver, you can't let guilt get the best of you.

In Chapter 2, we'll take a closer look at this powerful and often destructive, but sometimes useful, emotion. We'll talk about many ways to eliminate guilt and/or use it to your advantage.

Know When to Stop

When you become a caregiver, there's no rule that you have to be the sole caregiver indefinitely. When caregiving duties become more than you can bear or a family member requires medical attention or constant care that you simply can't provide, it's time to research other options. You may need to hold other family members accountable for a parent's care or check into assisted living centers or nursing homes.

When Lisa Keeler moved with her family to her husband's hometown in the picturesque foothills of the Great Smoky Mountains, she was looking for a simpler, laid-back lifestyle. She hadn't counted on becoming a caregiver to her husband's grandfather. "A year after we moved here, Pop had a stroke," she said. Though he was married at the time, his wife became tired of caregiving and left him six months later.

Without other family members nearby who were willing

and/or able to help, Keeler, her husband, and two children had to completely change their own family's lifestyle and move in with Pop. She and her husband, both emergency medical technicians, began working opposite shifts so that someone was always home with her grandfather-in-law. Later, the Keelers built rental cabins in the Smokies to supplement the family income, allowing Lisa to stay home more. Her husband took a job as a truck driver, which pays most of the family's bills, but keeps him on the road.

Today, ten years after she took on the job of caregiver, Keeler is looking forward to the day, in just a few more years, when another family member will take over the care of her grandfather-in-law, and she will have the opportunity to enjoy some time with her husband again. She advises caregivers to admit there are limits to what and how much they can do—and for how long.

"I am in the process of getting my CDL [truck drivers' license], so when our son graduates from high school, my husband and I are going to team up and travel," says Keeler. "I have already asked Pop's children to make arrangements, because by then I will have been taking care of him for thirteen years. It will be time for them to sacrifice some of their own time."

When you take on the care of a loved one, don't assume you've signed on for life. Certainly, you will always love your parents and you will want to help them and be with them as much as possible. But be willing to admit there may be a time when you can't always be there twenty-four hours a day or provide all of the care they need. When caregiving duties become more than you can handle, know when to say when.

See Chapter 3 for ways to gain the cooperation of family members and get them to shoulder some of the caregiving responsibility.

Go With the Flow

You planned to get a haircut today, but your mother broke a tooth and needs you to take her to the dentist. You wanted to get to work early to prepare for a presentation, but taking your father to his physical therapy appointment made you run *late* for work instead. You are preparing a nice dinner for your family when your parents call to say they need your help—right away.

Anyone who thinks life will go on as planned after they become a caregiver is in for a rude awakening. One of the most important attributes of an effective caregiver is flexibility.

In extreme cases, becoming a caregiver means being willing to make major changes in your lifestyle and daily routine. In most cases, it means making yourself available—often at the drop of the hat—in the event of any crisis that might arise.

Being flexible means being able to roll with the punches and understanding that, as a caregiver, you won't always be able to do the things you plan and want to do at the precise times you plan or want to do them. If you have always expected perfection from yourself and others, being flexible means being willing to lower your expectations sometimes. For example, if an afternoon call from your mother's doctor keeps you from getting a roast in the oven in time for dinner, frozen fish sticks may have to do.

Gail Kort learned the importance of flexibility in her fifty-plus years as a caregiver. "If you don't get the floor clean or the carpet sweeper run today, it will still be there tomorrow. Don't fret over the small stuff."

Take It as a Wake-Up Call

Though you may feel young, energetic, and in great health now, caring for an aging loved one can provide a sobering lesson that life can change quickly—and often in ways you would never choose. But rather than worry about what could or may happen, caregivers who have been there recommend heeding the lesson to prepare for your own future and to appreciate and make the most of the life you have now.

Gema Hernandez, former secretary of the Florida Department of Elder Affairs, got a lesson in how quickly and unpredictably life can change when her father was admitted to the hospital with kidney failure. Until that morning, Hernandez's parents had helped her with her own family—driving her kids to school or to doctors' appointments or occasionally picking up a much-needed gallon of milk from the grocery store.

When Hernandez's father began kidney dialysis, she thought his medical problems were under control and that, aside from having to go for his regular treatments, life would go on as it had in the past. "I thought that in a couple of days things would get back to normal, and I could get back to my routine of asking 'Papi' and 'Mami' to baby-sit for me," she says.

But that was not to be. Looking back, Hernandez realized that this fateful day marked the end of a time when she could call on her parents for help and the beginning of her own eighteen years as a caregiver.

Hernandez says being a caregiver has taught her never to take for granted the health she has, the mobility she possesses, and the agility of her mind. "It has taught me to live my life every day to its fullest, because retirement may or may not be as I have planned. Being a caregiver has given me a different outlook on life and more patience, more compassion, more respect for our elders, and more courage to fight for other caregivers like myself."

If you see an elderly family member struggle with illness and limitations every day, allow yourself to *learn* from the situation—learn love and compassion (you could well be in her position one day), and learn to appreciate the life you have and make the most of it now. For some fun and practical suggestions on how to make the most of your life now and in the years to come, see Chapter 7.

Seek the Support of Others

A joy shared is a joy doubled. A problem shared is a problem divided. As much as you may need the hands-on help of others in managing the physical and logistical aspects of caregiving, you need emotional support just as much (or more). When the stresses of caregiving seem just too much to bear, nothing helps like talking over your troubles with a sympathetic friend.

Bottling up your emotions can lead to burnout and health problems. Says Linda Dano, "Talking is very important. [Caregivers] must talk; share their emotions, their fear and their anger. They must talk."

While many people find comfort in talking informally with friends, others benefit from joining support groups made up of people facing similar challenges. And don't think a support group is just a big "pity party". In addition to sharing frustrations and sorrows, people in support groups share ideas for caregiving and coping. Some share caregiving duties or make themselves available to others in the event of an emergency. Some members form friendships that last long after their caregiving duties have ended. Most of all, anyone who goes to a support group receives the assurance that they are not alone.

In addition to finding friends and/or support groups with whom you can share, you might want to speak with a professional. When Peri Gilpin's mother was dying of breast cancer, Gilpin went to therapy. "I was in therapy for the last few months, so that I would have a good place to go and unload," she says. "For me, that was a good thing."

For information on how and where to find caregiver support groups, see "Attend a Support Group" in Chapter 7.

Take Pleasure in the Simple Things

Caring for a parent can disrupt plans and long-term goals. You may have to forgo a long-planned family vacation, postpone the purchase of a new home, pass on a job promotion, or wait a while longer to go back to school or take a second honeymoon. Because caregiving can make a big difference in your daily life, now it's more important than ever to take pleasure in little things: an unusually pretty fall morning, a phone call from a friend you haven't heard from in years, a five-dollar bill in the pocket of last year's winter coat, a two-for-one sale on your favorite brand of ice cream, or a spontaneous hug from your teenage son.

Being a caregiver is a serious job, but it shouldn't be all hard work and drudgery. Every day, try to find *something* to celebrate, and then treat the day as a special occasion. "One day my dad's sister stopped by for a visit at lunchtime. My mother and I were eating sandwiches and potato chips, but were pouring hot tea from her good wedding china," says Kort. "We got her fancy teapot out of the china cabinet in the middle of the day to enjoy—just the two of us."

What may have looked a bit crazy to Kort's aunt made perfect sense to Kort and her mother. If you wait for a special occasion to do something special, that occasion may never come.

Do at least one thing to make each day special. Wear a pretty sweater or apply your makeup, even when you have nowhere to go; rent a favorite book on CD or audiotape to listen to while you run errands in the car; set a pretty dinner table (you may even want to light candles); try a new hairstyle or lipstick color; or look up an old friend and send her a thinking-of-you card. Display something in your home that reminds you of happier, simpler times—a collection of Mickey Mouse memorabilia from your childhood, a vase of flowers like your mother used to grow in her garden, a favorite chair that was once in your grandmother's living room.

Life is short and it doesn't always turn out the way we plan. Learn to enjoy the simple things.

So there you have it! Words of wisdom from people who have cared for aging family members and lived to tell about it. From government officials and Hollywood celebrities to homemakers and hospital workers, their stories—and their advice—are much the same. But theirs are just a few of the many caregiver experiences you'll read about in this book. Throughout each chapter, you'll find snippets of stories from women—and sometimes men—faced with the difficult, yet often rewarding, tasks of caregiving. These survival tips are just an entrée to what's ahead—six more chapters to teach, inspire, enlighten, and yes, sometimes even entertain you.

Note: Celebrity quotes were provided by the Caregiver Media Group, publishers of Today's Caregiver *magazine, Gary Barg, Publisher, www.caregiver.com.*

Two

WHY DO I FEEL SO GUILTY?

When you took on the job of caregiver, you probably knew you'd go through times of sadness, fear, uncertainty, and sheer exhaustion.

But many women tell me they are plagued by a feeling they never expected—guilt. I've heard countless women say that regardless of how much they do for their parents, they always feel as if they could be doing more.

Though feelings of guilt can be troubling and hard to shake, they are perfectly understandable. Raised in an age when our mothers sacrificed freedom and careers for their families, we somehow feel obligated to do the same for them. Unfortunately, as we all eventually discover, doing so is impossible.

While rearing us was probably our mothers' main responsibility—if not their only one—taking care of an elderly mother and/or father is just one of many responsibilities of today's family caregiver. The typical caregiver today is a forty-six-year-old married woman with a job outside of the home. Almost half of the women who care for their aging parents also have children under eighteen still living at home. Squeezed between two generations needing and demanding their care, these women are often referred to collectively as the "sandwich generation." One woman, who was caring for both her parents and two teenage girls, told me her life was like one of those big overstuffed sandwiches you have to end up eating with a fork. "My life is too full," she told me. "Sometimes I can hardly hold it all together."

The Guilt Trap

Overwhelmed by the scope of what they have to do for bosses, spouses, children, and the other people in their lives, caregivers feel torn. If this sounds like you, you may be feeling that you're cheating everyone, including yourself, of time and attention; hence your feelings of guilt.

Guilt can also be a result of anger—anger over what you've lost. Perhaps you've had to give up your free time, vacations with your family, or your favorite hobbies in exchange for caregiving duties. Perhaps you've given up promotions, life savings, or your 401(K) to provide care for your parents. Maybe you've been forced to choose between attending your child's parent-teacher conference or taking Dad to the doctor. Or perhaps you've had business meetings interrupted by calls from your mother, saying she needs you—now!

Even as you do—and do—for your aging parents, they or other family members may complain or insinuate you aren't doing an adequate amount. That's enough to make anyone angry. On the other hand, your parent may have asked or expected very little help from you. Maybe what makes you angry is that *she* can no longer take care of *you*.

The Risks of Guilt

Regardless of the reasons for anger or guilt, dwelling on these feelings helps no one. Focusing on negative feelings takes our attention from positive action, from doing the best we can for our elderly parents and ourselves. Doing more for your parent to assuage the guilt that comes with anger can only lead to more anger. Mistaken feelings of "I should be doing more" can lead us to the point of exhaustion and depression.

If your caregiving duties have you overwhelmed and exhausted, you're not alone. In a survey by the National Family Caregivers Association, 25 percent of caregivers reported feeling "out of control" and "emotional stress," and 61 percent reported that they became more depressed after assuming the caregiving role. Indeed, some 13 percent of caregivers admitted to having formulated a suicide plan for themselves.

While plans of suicide are certainly the extreme—and, fortunately, few people who contemplate suicide actually follow through—a great many caregivers do suffer physiological effects of stress that threaten their health and their lives in other ways. Research in recent years has suggested that psychological stress can cause increased levels of certain hormones that can lead to health problems. If you care for a loved one with dementia, one study suggests you're likely to have higher levels of the hormone cortisol—which puts you at increased risk of health problems such as heart disease and some cancers.

Studies also show that the depression that often results from caregiving can lead to changes in the body's immune system as well, possibly leaving you less able to fight infections and cancer. And when compared to the general population, caregivers are more likely to rate their health as only fair to poor. Clearly, a caregiver caught in the cycle of guilt, anger, and depression may leave herself vulnerable to serious health problems that would actually prevent her from providing the best care for the ones she loves. However you look at it, too much stress is bad for you. Don't risk your own life, and health, for others.

Before we go further, just one note of caution: If you're starting to feel bad about how your guilt may be hurting yourself and your loved one, recognize one thing—guilt is a feeling, and feelings aren't inherently right or wrong. Acting on negative feelings, however, can be wrong. If you allow your feelings of guilt and anger to affect your behavior toward your parent (for example, by becoming physically or emotionally abusive), obviously, that *is* wrong. It's also wrong to let feelings of guilt rob you of your own health or of the joy of your own life.

Seeing your parent aging and ill should be a wake-up call. Life is short. Good health is a blessing. While it is natural to be concerned for your parent(s), don't allow your caregiving role to consume you. Do what you can to take care of your own

✐ The Martyr Syndrome

Be careful not to become a martyr. You know the type of person I'm talking about: She suffers and sacrifices her own life with the expectation of instilling admiration, guilt, or pity in others. But in the end, the martyr helps no one—including herself. People rarely admire a martyr—they're more likely to be irritated by her "woe is me" attitude and inability to share her responsibilities. All the while, the martyr sacrifices to the detriment of her own health. Only by eliminating guilt can you avoid damage to your relationship and your health.

health. Take time to enjoy life. And, as much as you can, enjoy these remaining days, months, or years with the loved one you care for.

Freeing Yourself from the Guilt

On the following pages you'll learn ten guidelines for caregiving that will help you free yourself from the guilt and allow you to take better care of your loved ones *and* yourself.

1. *Acknowledge Your Feelings*

Feelings are simply that—feelings. Nothing more. Nothing less. When you're caring for aging parents, however, some feelings are hard to accept. Having negative feelings about caregiving *does not* make you a bad caregiver. Mistakenly, we sometimes see these conflicted feelings as signs that we are self-centered, immature, or not up to the task of caregiving.

One of the most common and bothersome feelings caregivers experience is anger. And no wonder. Taking care of an aging parent is a job you never asked for, and it is probably affecting all areas of your life. Perhaps you've had to forego family vacations or give up lazy Saturdays with your spouse. You may have had to turn your family room into a bedroom for your parents, build an expensive addition onto your house, give up job promotions (or your job itself), or deplete your bank account for long-term care expenses. On the other hand, you might not have done any of these things. What makes you angry may simply be the fact that your parents can no longer do things for *you*.

Whatever the cause of your anger, it can easily turn into guilt—if you let it. After all, you ask yourself, how can you be angry with someone for growing old and needing your help? Certainly they never asked to be in this situation either.

It's important to know that feelings—including negative ones such as anger—are natural. In and of themselves, feelings are not bad. The way you act on your feelings, however, can be. Letting your anger affect the way you treat your parents—such as snapping at them or putting them down—understandably can cause hurt feelings. Allowing anger to lead to guilt and then letting guilt get in the way of caring for yourself is unhealthy for you.

The best way to deal with anger is to acknowledge it, accept it as a perfectly legitimate feeling, and then move on. If you have an open relationship with your parents and can talk about your feelings, you'll probably learn that you are not alone in your anger. They're probably feeling angry, too—at the "times" for changing, at their bodies (and perhaps their minds) for failing them, or at friends or family members for dying or abandoning them. They may even be angry with you for reasons they can't fully understand or explain.

If anger becomes a constant feeling or if it causes you to treat your loved one badly, it's important to seek professional help immediately. A mental health professional can help you identify the source of your anger (it may go deeper than the current demands of your parents) and how to deal with it.

To find a mental health professional who can help you deal with anger, check with a local caregiving organization, your family doctor (or your parents' doctor, since you are probably there regularly), friends or coworkers, or your place of worship for recommendations. You may also check out some of the following Web sites for listings of professionals in your area: www.helphorizons.com/counselor, www.athealth.com, and www.find-a-therapist.com.

2. Think Quality, Not Quantity

With all of our responsibilities to our jobs, our families, our communities, and ourselves, it is often difficult to spend all of our time with our aging parents, but it's important to make the most of the time we have. To borrow an overused phrase from the child care debate of the 1980s, we can have "quality time" without "quantity time."

Nancy discovered the importance of spending quality time with her father after her mother died. At age eighty, her father was left to fend for himself for the first time in his life. He had never run a vacuum cleaner, washed his own laundry, or, for that matter, cleaned the bathroom. And furthermore, he made it clear he wasn't about to start!

Although Nancy lived thirty miles away and had a family and a full-time job, she offered to help him with his meals and housekeeping. She spent much of her weekends doing his laundry and preparing meals he could freeze and reheat. Twice a week, she made the trip to his house—often after a full workday—to pick up or drop off laundry, deliver his meals, wash a load of dishes, or give the house a quick cleaning. For bigger chores, like errands and her father's doctors' appointments, she took leave from work.

After a year of this taxing routine, Nancy was exhausted. Her husband, who had looked forward to spending more time with her after their youngest child left for college, was jealous of the time she spent with her father. As Nancy's husband became more irritable, Nancy became more impatient with her father. If her father suggested she sit and watch a TV show with him or help with a crossword puzzle, she snapped at him. Wasn't she doing enough already?

Later, feeling guilty over her displays of anger, she made an important realization: While she was dutifully racking up hours and miles doing chores for her father, she had really become nothing more than a maid. She wasn't truly caring for him. In other words, she was giving him quantity time but not quality time. Once she made that important discovery, she got on the phone and began looking for housekeepers and home-health aids to fill those roles.

Although her father grumbled at first about the "hired help," he came to enjoy the extra attention he got from Nancy when she wasn't busy loading his freezer or scrubbing his bathtub. In time, Nancy was able to let go of the guilt of "not doing it all herself."

Today, at eighty-three, her father is still in his own home. Nancy visits twice a week and spends her visits doing things her father appreciates most—cheering on his favorite football team or listening to his World War II stories. She still takes him to doctors' appointments and, occasionally, she cooks a pot of his favorite chili. But jokingly, she says, "I don't do windows anymore."

By helping your parent get the help they need—but not necessarily doing it all yourself—you'll have time for things that probably mean more to them than a scrubbed bathtub or freshly dusted furniture. As a result, you and your parent will enjoy your time together more, and you'll free up time to nurture yourself and the other relationships in your life.

3. Establish Priorities

Some people may have more energy, more help, or more money than others, but we all have the same number of hours each day to get things done. Often we must divide those hours among many commitments—husbands, kids, jobs, community service, and, if we are wise, our own interests. Yet a family member often makes requests, and sometimes demands, as if they are our only responsibility or there are no limits to how much we can do. Often we make those same demands on ourselves. If we go into caregiving with the mindset that we are Superwoman (able to do everything for everybody and leap over tall buildings to boot), our physical and emotional health will eventually prove us wrong.

While no one can do everything, most women can find the time and muster the energy to do the things that are most important to them. But doing so requires establishing priorities—determining which things in your life are most worthy of your time and energy and then planning your time accordingly. That way, the most important tasks get completed and the most important needs get met.

Many people don't consciously establish priorities. A teenager who spends every waking minute at the mall with friends instead of studying or doing her chores, for example, probably doesn't put a lot of effort into deciding what should take priority in her life—she just does what she enjoys. Neither does a husband who routinely sits in front of the TV all weekend while his wife cooks, cleans, and cares for the kids—he does what comes easily with little concern for his responsibilities. Yet in both cases, it's clear where their priorities lie.

For responsible adults who don't have the luxury of endless mall-strolling or TV viewing, establishing priorities often requires a more systematic approach. Try setting priorities by writing down first what you feel you *must* do each week and second what you would *like to* do each week. (Be sure to add time for yourself in the "must" category.) Now, plug each item into a weekly schedule, making sure you allot enough time to each activity on this list. (I discovered long ago that

✐ Honor Yourself

As caregivers, we must honor ourselves, something that we at times neglect to do. After all, from our earliest memories, we have always been told to honor our mother and father. Unfortunately, many of us believe that honoring our mother and father somehow means neglecting our own wants and needs. But is that what our parents really want for us? Is working yourself to the point of exhaustion and despair really honoring your parents?

By honoring your own needs, you are not only achieving your parents' goal for your life (most parents want what's best for their children, don't they?), you're also keeping yourself healthy and sane so that you can take care of them.

If you have children of your own, remember that your behavior toward your parents now will be a model for how your kids will act toward you someday, if they're confronted with the same situation. Wouldn't you want your children to help you out of love but still take time to nourish their own lives, rather than serving you hand and foot—with anger and resentment building all the way?

For most parents, the goal of raising children is to make them self-sufficient to pursue their own goals and dreams—not to be slaves to caring for their parents. Thinking of your children can help you focus on the role you should play in your parents' care. Remember they are watching you.

most tasks take 50 percent longer than I expect them to.) Also schedule some time between activities to allow for traffic, long checkout lines, unforeseen delays, or just a little breathing room.

If you can't fit everything neatly into your schedule, look for areas to cut—and not just from the "like to do" section. With some thought and creativity, you may realize that you really don't have to do everything on your "must" list. Perhaps you could free up time in other ways. Some of the following may help:

CONSOLIDATE ERRANDS

Avoid multiple car trips when possible. Plan your meals and make a grocery list once a week (if you shop for your parents, do their shopping at the same time). If possible, buy your groceries, medications, cleaning supplies, and postage stamps all in one store. In some larger stores, you can bank and pick up your dry cleaning as well.

MAKE USE OF DOWNTIME

Though you feel like you're always rushing here and there, you may have more downtime than you realize—while waiting for your son to finish soccer practice, the mechanic to change your oil, or your mother to complete a medical test, for example. Rather than stress out about what you could or should be doing, use the time to your advantage. Write checks, compose thank-you notes, address birthday cards, fill out insurance forms, or make an important phone call.

Alternatively, you can use the time for relaxation. Bring along a favorite book, magazine, or a CD in a portable player. Or use the time to just sit and do absolutely nothing (including worrying about how late you will be to your next appointment). I know this is hard but, just like your body, your *mind* must also rest. Taking a break for nothing but pure relaxation can help make you resilient, strong, and better able to face the responsibilities of caregiving.

GET YOUR SPOUSE, SIBLINGS, AND KIDS TO HELP

Sure, having a family adds to your responsibilities, but they can also be a solution to your time crunch. Every family member should have roles of responsibility in the family. Perhaps your spouse or kids (depending on their ages) could help directly in the care of your parents. If not, they might take on more responsibility in your home—helping with laundry, meal preparation, or vacuuming, for example. Their help with household tasks will free up time for you. (For more on how you can get family members to help, see Chapter 3.)

MAKE CHANGES AT WORK

If you have a full-time job, it is probably your single most time-consuming responsibility. Yet there are ways you may be able to reduce your work time or make it more efficient.

- *Flex-time* (working hours other than the traditional nine to five), for example, may enable you to work the same number of hours while avoiding commutes during heavy traffic. In a major metropolitan area, that alone could save you two or more hours a day.

- *Telecommuting* (essentially working from home, at least some days) could save you the commute time *and* the need to wear panty hose!

- *Part-time* work is definitely an option worth considering if your employer offers it and you find that working full-time is no longer possible. But before you cut back your work hours, be sure to consider the financial consequences of such a move. Not only will you make less, you may also give up benefits, such as health insurance, paid vacation, and retirement. While you want to care for your parents, it's also important that you have the resources to care for yourself.

In some cases, it's possible to get paid to be your parent's caregiver. To learn more about that option and other important information on careers and caregiving, see Chapter 6.

HIRE A PROFESSIONAL

Providing care for your parents doesn't have to mean physically doing it all yourself. For a fee, many people will provide services such as shopping, light housekeeping, and taking your parents to doctors' appointments. Home-health nurses, physical therapists, and other health professionals provide medical services right in your family member's home. For more information on how to find a home-health professional, check out the Eldercare Locator at (800) 677-1116 or online at www.eldercare.gov or visit the National Association of Area Agencies on Aging at www.n4a.org.

ADJUST THE EXPECTATIONS YOU PUT ON YOURSELF AND YOUR FAMILY

Of course, you'd like for your family (both immediate and your parents) to live in a spotless home, eat a home-cooked meal each evening, and wear clean, pressed clothes every day. But if you expect to make all these things happen, you're probably expecting too much. When faced with high expectations, ask yourself, "Will a little dust, frozen pizza, or wash-and-wear clothes really hurt every now and then?" If not (the *right* answer), then simply resolve to do the best you can and move forward.

Once you've created your weekly schedule of priorities, let it serve as your guide. But also feel free to make changes as *necessary*. The only thing worse than not having a plan is following your plan too rigidly. Make allowances for downtime and the flexibility for emergencies. For example, while it may be a priority for your mother to get to her weekly bingo game, she'll obviously need to forego bingo one day if your daughter's school calls to inform you that she has broken her arm on the playground. Likewise, while getting your son to Cub Scouts may be a priority, he may need to miss a meeting or two if your father has emergency surgery.

When you're pulled in many different directions, setting priorities can be difficult. But in the long run, it's a lot more productive—and a lot less stressful—than trying to handle everything that comes your way all at once and then feeling guilty about what you don't accomplish.

4. Set Limits

Do you feel like you're doing everything you humanly can, yet people keep expecting you to do more? Do you often feel guilty when you can't meet unrealistic demands? If so, it's time you took a lesson in acknowledging and setting limits. As the familiar drug campaign reminds us, we must learn to "just say no."

Many women with busy lives don't realize the importance—indeed the necessity—of setting limits until the demands of caregiving stretch them to the breaking point. Such was the case with Barbara, a woman who approached me after a keynote speech I gave to members of a caregivers organization.

Like many wives and mothers, Barbara was always busy. If her son's class needed costumes for the school play, Barbara sewed them. If her daughter's Girl Scout troop held a cookie sale, Barbara coordinated it. If her husband wanted to entertain a client, Barbara cleaned the house or purchased the theater tickets.

Barbara's busy life suited her just fine until her aging parents started demanding more and more of her time. Having always thrived on being busy and feeling needed, she approached her new caregiving tasks enthusiastically—at least, at first.

But her parents, knowing that they could always count on Barbara, began to call her for everything—from picking up a loaf of bread to replacing a lightbulb to opening the child-proof cap on their arthritis medication. If Barbara wasn't able to act immediately, she imagined her parents hungry, sitting in the dark, and behind on their medications.

As their calls became more frequent—often several times a day—it became evident that it wasn't Barbara's help they needed, but her attention. Run ragged by their constant demands, Barbara had to do something she had never done before—she set limits.

Similar to establishing priorities, setting limits requires acknowledging that you can't do everything and then deciding—and letting your parents know—just how much you are able and willing to do.

The first thing Barbara did was to get her parents organized—with enough food to last several days; extra batteries, lightbulbs, and paper supplies in the pantry; and a week's worth of medications set out in a labeled, easy-open container. Since she lived close to her parents, she agreed to visit or run errands for them twice a week on the days of their choosing. Beyond that, she would come only for a true emergency.

For a while, her parents protested and Barbara continued to feel guilty, but in time everyone became more comfortable with the routine. Her parents saved up requests for her twice-weekly visits and Barbara, understanding her parents' craving for her attention—and not stressed-out and guilt-ridden by her inability to meet their incessant demands—gradually began spending more quality time with her parents and enjoying the visits more.

If your parents are making constant or unreasonable demands, it's essential to say "no" sometimes. While it's important that you are always available in the event of a true emergency, there are probably many "crises" you can avert with a little planning. Plus, your parents can probably do more for themselves than they think—especially if you're not running to help them every time they call. Let your parents know what you are able and willing to do to help them—and then stick to your guns. It may take a while for everyone to get used to your limits—particularly if you have always said "yes" to their every request—but in the long run, everyone will benefit.

5. Redefine Your Concept of Caring

Sometimes we feel guilty because we don't have warm and fuzzy feelings about caring for our parents or providing hands-on help for them. If that rings true for you, don't beat yourself up over it. Caring for a parent doesn't mean you have to coddle them or even feel affection for them (although I am sure it would be much appreciated)—you just have to behave responsibly toward them. Many times the way we feel about and treat our parents has a lot to do with how they felt about and treated us when we were young.

I made this important realization during a recent cab ride. While en route to the airport, I struck up a conversation with the driver—a man who grew up in South America but moved to New York as a young adult. He said he had recently moved with his mother and family to sunny L.A. because his mom couldn't stand the cold New York winters.

I was touched that a grown man would be so concerned

about his mother that he would be willing to move his entire family across the country for her comfort and well-being. I asked him if it had been a difficult decision. He told me no, that self-sacrifice for a family member was not unusual in his culture.

"It's much different from here," he said. "Americans are so eager to push their kids out the door once they're eighteen. So why should children feel a responsibility to their parents later in life?"

While I understood his point, I had mixed feelings about what he said. Helping children become independent, self-sufficient adults should be a goal of parents everywhere. If a man (or woman) is able-bodied and capable of holding a job, there's absolutely no reason his parents should be supporting him financially, doing his laundry, and preparing his meals when he's forty. In fact, there are plenty of good reasons why parents shouldn't allow this codependence to take place.

On the other hand, I do agree with his assessment that many families push their children to be independent too soon. What he failed to mention was all of the others who leave the day-to-day care of their children to nannies or other relatives, believing their greatest contribution to their family is an expensive home, nice cars, or trendy clothing. As a result, they fail to bond with their children emotionally.

One key to caregiving lies in having good role models. If your parents treated you with warmth and affection, chances are you will want to treat them the same way. On the other hand, if they were rarely present or overly eager to get you out of the house, you probably don't feel very loving toward them now. But unless you understand why you feel the way you do, your ambivalence may lead to feelings of guilt and anger.

It's important to understand that feelings of affection aren't necessary to be a good caregiver. Nor does the lack of such feelings give you an excuse not to care for your parents. Like it or not, family members have a *responsibility* to one another. But not all caregivers are hands-on caregivers. Many women care for family members in distant cities, coordinating doctors and medications by phone, handling their parents' finances, or hiring professionals to handle the day-to-day hands-on care.

If you think caregiving means you must feel loving and provide hands-on care, it may help to reconsider your definition of caring. People care—and show their care—for one another in different ways. I have often heard that love is not how you feel but what you do. The same can be said of caring. It's not just a nice feeling. It's what you do for your elderly parent—making sure they have medical care, nourishment, and a safe comfortable place to live—not whether you provide these things directly.

6. Act from Love, Not from a Sense of Debt

While most of us feel a responsibility to our aging parents, caring for our parents should be viewed as a labor of love, not as repayment of a debt. If you go into caregiving with the goal of repaying your parents for all they've done for you, *you're destined to fail*. Feelings of failure can lead to guilt, as my friend Carol can attest to.

All her life, Carol had been close to her mother. When she was a little girl and fell off her bike, her mother was always there to help her up; if she had a bad dream, her mother rushed to comfort her. As a teenager, if Carol wanted to go to the mall or a movie with her friends, her mother was the one to drive them; when she played on her high school basketball team, her mother never missed a game. When a boyfriend broke up with Carol, her mother was there to pick up the pieces.

Years later, when Carol's mother suffered fractures of her spine, Carol couldn't do enough for her. "All my life, she has cared for me so much, now it's my turn to repay her," she said. What Carol eventually came to realize is that no matter how much she did for her mother, she could never repay her hour-for-hour, hug-for-hug, or tear-for-tear for all that her mother had done for her.

At age forty, Carol had other responsibilities competing for her time—a seven-year-old son, a husband, a part-time job, and a volunteer position with her neighborhood association. Caring for her mother became taxing, and the demands of her family and job vied for her attention. Carol felt discouraged and, yes, guilty.

I encouraged Carol to view her caregiving tasks in a new light. "Think of each thing you do for your mother not as payment toward a huge, looming debt, but as a positive step toward providing for her care."

Once Carol was able to see her caregiving as an opportunity to help her mother instead of as a debt to repay, she was able to relax and feel better about what she was doing rather than feeling guilty about what she couldn't do.

7. Forgive and Seek Forgiveness

While Carol's relationship for her mother had always been a loving one, not all parent-child relationships are. Sometimes, we have to get past feelings of regret or resentment before we can be effective caregivers.

Trudy, a woman whom I spoke with recently, told me that a grudge she had held against her mother for more than three decades had made it hard for her to care for her mother in her final years. Even though Trudy's mother had treated her kindly when she was a child, the woman dutifully stood by Trudy's alcoholic father while he physically and emotionally abused Trudy and her three older sisters. "I used to pray at night that my mother would divorce my father, but she stayed with him until the day his drinking finally killed him," she told me.

The month after her father died, Trudy graduated from high school and moved out of state to live with one of her sisters. She rarely spoke with her mother and often went a year or two without seeing her—until one morning almost twenty years later, when Trudy's mother called to tell her she had been diagnosed with ovarian cancer. The prognosis was not good.

Because Trudy was the only one of the four sisters without a spouse and children of her own, she decided she was the logical choice to care for their mother. So she quit her job, sold the condo she had saved dearly for, and moved back into the house where she had grown up. She served as chauffeur, cook, and housekeeper for her mother while she underwent painful treatments that left her sick, weak, and without hair. "Sometimes I wondered why I was doing all of this for her when she never did anything to protect me from my father," she recalled.

At the same time, Trudy felt guilty about all of the years she had stayed away from her mother, with rarely even a phone call. Somehow she had always felt her mother would be there when she was ready to forgive her, but her mother's illness made her realize that life is short. The years she missed were ones she could never make up. One afternoon, as she sat by her mother's side during a chemotherapy treatment, tears came to Trudy's eyes. She asked her mother to forgive her.

Trudy longed for an apology from her mother, but one never came. In time, Trudy came to realize that her mother was just a woman with human frailties—a woman who wanted a man to love her and a father (if not a good father) for her children.

Once Trudy decided to forgive her mother—with or without an apology—her feelings of anger and guilt began to ease, and caring for her mother became less of a chore.

If you truly feel like you have done something to hurt your parent, and your feelings of guilt are hindering your ability to care for him or her or live with yourself, ask for forgiveness and move on. You can't undo what's been done, but you can resolve to do things differently in the future.

If your parent has done things that have hurt you, try to find it in your heart to forgive—for your own sake. I once read that holding a grudge is like taking poison and hoping the other person gets sick. The anger and guilt that result from not forgiving ultimately hurt you.

8. Foster Their Independence

As caregivers, we sometimes feel guilty for all of the things we don't do for our parents. What you may not realize or be willing to admit is that your parents, with a little encouragement and the right tools, could probably do many more things for themselves.

Consider the importance of one simple device—a pill dispenser with an alarm—in Jana's relationship with her father. Not long ago, Jana routinely made lists of all the medications her father was supposed to take and the times he was supposed to take them. She kept the lists with her at all times and, each day, wherever she happened to be when it was time for him to take a medication, she called to remind him.

After a while, the calls became tedious for Jana and her father grew tired of her "nagging." Jana figured there had to be a better way. While speaking with her father's pharmacist, she learned about a pill dispenser with an alarm that she could set when it was time for her father to take his medications. She could fill the dispenser at the first of each week and trust the device—and her father—to do the rest.

So far, the plan has worked out well. Jana's father is proud of his ability to handle his own medications, and Jana brags on her father for taking his medication instead of nagging him to take it. Furthermore, she is relieved of the burden of having to make the constant phone calls and the guilt that would result if she occasionally missed a call.

In Chapter 5, I talk about many tips and devices for helping your parents become more independent. Helping and encouraging your parents to do what they can is a win-win situation. They will thrive on the feeling of independence, and you will have more time for *you*.

9. *Face the Facts*

At some point there may come a time when you simply can't handle the full brunt of caregiving—for your for parents' sake, as well as your own.

Anita was a forty-year-old mother of five-year-old twins and caregiver to her seventy-seven-year-old widowed father with Alzheimer's when she had to face the fact that she could no longer care for her father in her home. Just two years earlier he had come to live with her family and, at first, Anita managed pretty well. Her father sat in front of the TV most days and required less supervision than her active twins. But as her father's condition deteriorated further, it became obvious that Anita was essentially acting as a mother for three small children.

By the time the twins started kindergarten, her father was clearly the most needy of the three. Anita's children had barely gotten past the stage of requiring constant attention when her father entered that stage. "I felt like I had a toddler again, only this time it was harder," Anita said. "He pulled heavy items off shelves, roamed the house at all hours of the night, and put small objects in his mouth."

One morning, fearing that her father might have swallowed a paper clip that had held the twins' school papers together the night before, Anita took him to the doctor to have his stomach x-rayed. There, the doctor found a small assortment of items—the paper clip as well as a penny and a safety pin (fortunately it was closed!).

Although all three objects eventually passed without causing lasting harm, the incident was a wake-up call to Anita. She realized she could no longer keep her father safe. The tactics that had worked with her kids—such as putting off-limits items on high shelves or punishing them if they left their rooms at night—were not practical for her father.

Eventually, she admitted her father to a nursing home, where he could be under constant supervision. Although she frequently felt pangs of guilt after making the decision, in her heart she knew it was for the best. She had more time to devote to her husband and children, and she was able to visit her father as well. Most important, her father was well cared for in a safe environment.

Anita's father is among the estimated 5 percent of Americans over age sixty-five who live in institutional settings. Moving your loved one into an assisted living center or nursing home doesn't mean you have forgotten about or no longer want to care for them. Most people continue to stay close and emotionally involved with loved ones in nursing homes, and often they continue to provide such services as doing their loved one's laundry or arranging for a hairdresser to come in and wash and style their hair.

Sometimes you just have to face the fact that your elderly parent requires more care than you can give. Making a decision for your loved one's welfare should never be a cause for guilt.

Don't Go It Alone

When you're consumed with caring for a loved one, just taking the time to shower or shave your legs can feel like a luxury. It's no wonder women who care for elderly parents often feel overwhelmed.

One critical step to easing the stress—and guilt—of caregiving is to admit that you can't do it alone and to seek help. In many cases, other family members—including your own husband and children—may be able to share in the caregiving. (For more on how to get family members to help, see Chapter 3.) In other cases, you'll need to hire people to help with some care-giving tasks. Many caregivers rely on a combination of family and paid help. In fact, many women prefer to have paid caregivers take care of highly personal tasks such as bathing or getting them on and off the toilet.

As you consider people who help your loved one, don't forget the importance of being around people who can help *you*. Interacting with friends about issues other than caregiving is essential to your sanity. At the same time, talking to other caregivers can provide you with tips for coping and remind you that your feelings are perfectly normal.

Many organizations offer support groups for family caregivers. Research shows that taking part in a support group can help more than just your *mental* health. In fact, caregivers who seek emotional support—either in a group or one-on-one setting—are less likely to need health care themselves. One study showed that caregivers of elderly spouses who were involved in support groups had lower health care costs during a one-year period than did a group of caregivers not involved in support groups.

Typically, support groups are held at hospitals, places of worship, community centers, or assisted-living homes. Some meet weekly, some monthly, some during business hours, and others in the evening. Some allow your loved one to come along and join the group, if they are able. If you can't get away from your caregiving duties for even a short time, at least one national organization, the Alzheimer's Association, holds an evening telephone support group. Other state and local organizations offer telephone support groups for people who can't attend support groups or live in rural areas where they aren't available. For information on how to contact organizations that offer support groups, see page 225.

10. Don't Succumb to Peer Pressure

If you must make tough decisions for your parents, do your research, consider your options, trust your instincts, and stick to your choices! Chances are someone will come along who will plant a seed of doubt in your mind—if not blatantly accuse you of doing the wrong thing. When that happens, stand your ground. More important, don't feel guilty about the decision you've made.

Joann was a single, working mother with three teenagers when her seventy-nine-year-old mother suffered a series of strokes that left her needing round-the-clock care, which Joann could neither pay for nor provide herself. Joann began feeling pangs of guilt after she had made the only decision she felt she could for her aging mother.

"My time was stretched, my tiny three-bedroom house was bursting at the seams, and my paycheck barely covered the mortgage and utilities," Joann recalls. "I just couldn't handle another thing!"

Joann looked into her options and resources; she talked with her mother's doctor and a social worker at the hospital where her mother would soon be released. For a month following her mother's strokes, Joann did little but cry and consider her choices. When a nursing home she had inquired about called to tell her they had a Medicaid bed available, she felt a huge sense of relief—for a little while.

The following month was stressful as Joann used the annual leave from her job to clean and close her mother's apartment, sort through family mementos, and help her mother get situated in her new home. When Joann returned to work, she called her mother daily and fit in frequent visits between her sons' ball games and her daughter's orthodontist visits.

As the months wore on, Joann began to question her decision about her mother's care. A few "friends" fueled her doubts, by telling her they would never put *their* mothers in a nursing home. Others asked why she didn't have her mother move in with her.

With more people in her home than bedrooms already—and a job that kept her away all day—the answer seemed quite obvious to Joann. Yet her friends' comments hit a raw nerve. Perhaps she *could* be doing more, perhaps she *should* be.

When it comes to caregiving—whether for children or elderly parents—everyone's an expert. Often the biggest experts—at least, in their own eyes—are those who have never been care-givers themselves. Remember, even those who *have* been care-givers have never been in the exact same circumstances as you. Many people who criticize other people's choices do so because they are dealing with their own guilt issues. Your situation is unique, so go with your gut. If you are the primary caregiver, you are the only one with all the facts to make the right decisions for you and your family. The power of a woman's instinct is no joke!

Search Your Soul

Now that I have told you all of the reasons you *shouldn't* feel guilty, I think it's important to let you know there are cases when you *should* allow yourself feelings of guilt. In those cases, if you acknowledge and deal with the reasons for guilt early on, it can lead you to important and gratifying changes in the way you live your life as a caregiver—and possibly spare you even more guilt and regrets in the long run.

Take the story of a woman named Angela. Angela's father's fall couldn't have come at a worse time. She had been at her new job for just six months when she received the news that her father had slipped on his front-porch step and broken his hip.

For eighteen years Angela had prided herself on taking care of her family and had made the decision to not work outside the home. But with her son away at college, she felt she needed more in her life and ultimately began looking for an outside job. When she landed one, she completely immersed herself in it. She stayed so busy with her job that she scarcely had time to think about her father, much less take time off to see him.

Three weeks after the fall, when Angela's older sister called to tell her their father was suffering serious complications from a blood clot that formed after the surgery to repair his fractured hip, Angela was worried—would he survive? Would she have the chance to see him again? Most of all, she felt confusion and guilt—why hadn't she taken the time to be with him immedeatly after his fall?

For eighteen years Angela had considered herself a loving, caring person whose *preference* was always to put her family over a job. Her behavior since her father's fall had been inconsistent with her true self and her *true* desires. Even though her son didn't need her ongoing attention, someone else in her life did, and that was where she wanted to be.

The inconsistency between Angela's actions and her "true self" were the cause of her guilt. Psychologists tell us that when our behaviors and values don't mesh, we feel bad—and perhaps we should. In these cases, feelings of guilt warrant some questions to ourselves, if not all-out soul-searching about the true reasons behind decisions we have made.

If you find that there's a legitimate reason for your guilt—perhaps you have neglected your responsibility to your parent—think of what you can do to change the situation. You can't undo what you've done in the past, but you can strive to do better. But that's not to say you should necessarily do more. Constantly doing more to relieve your feelings of guilt can lead to fatigue, feelings of being used, anger, and more guilt.

After some soul-searching, Angela decided that taking the needed time to be with her father was worth the risk it might pose to her job. She took off the time she needed to care for her father during the most critical days of his illness and then to help him make the transition from the hospital to an assisted-living home. When she returned home, her job was waiting.

Angela no longer neglects her father. It has been three years since her father was hospitalized for the blood clot. She calls him frequently and she and her family visit him almost every month. "When my dad had the blood clot, I realized I couldn't take one day of his life for granted," Angela says. "I'm making the most of my second chance with him. I don't want to look back someday with regrets."

Are you feeling guilty because your actions are inconsistent with your values? If so, don't dwell on your guilt, but resolve to make changes, as Angela did, before it's too late.

While guilt can be unsettling, it's important to understand that it's a common emotion. If past wrongs are causing you to feel guilty now, do your best to make amends, gain closure, and move on! If the inability to do all things for all people is the source of your guilt, wake up. No one—not even you—can do the impossible. Getting help from others will lighten both your load and your heart. In Chapter 3, we'll discover ways to get others to share the responsibilities of caregiving.

❧ Getting Free of Guilt's Grip ❧
Ten tips to help you say good-bye to guilt

1. *Acknowledge your feelings.* Negative feelings can make us feel uneasy and guilty, but it's important to understand that feelings of anger and resentment are natural and common. Unless these feelings control us, and our behavior toward our parents, they are not bad.

2. *Think quality, not quantity.* If you're feeling guilty because you aren't spending enough time with your parents, think of how you can improve the *quality* of your time together. Spending time reminiscing with your mother or playing a game of checkers with your father, for example, may mean more than cleaning their kitchen or delivering a pot roast.

3. *Establish priorities.* While no one has the time or energy to do *everything* for *everybody,* you must find time (and energy) to do the things that are most important to you. By establishing priorities—and allowing some flexibility for the unexpected—you can help ensure that the most important needs are met and the most important tasks get done.

4. *Set limits.* If your parents' constant demands are running you ragged, decide and clearly acknowledge what you are able and willing to do for them. By setting limits and standing behind them, you can help reduce the guilt trips that come when you can't meet their every demand.

5. *Redefine your concept of caring.* If you find it difficult to provide loving, hands-on care for your parent, don't feel guilty—simply think of other tangible ways you can help provide for his or her care.

6. *Act from love, not from a sense of debt.* If you think of caring for a parent as repayment for all he or she's done for you, you'll always end up in the red. Instead, think of caregiving as one person helping another out of love.

7. *Forgive and seek forgiveness.* If your parent was abusive or uncaring when you were a child, now is the time to forgive—even if you truly feel he or she doesn't deserve it. Holding grudges will not only affect your ability to care for your parent, but it will also hurt *you.*

8. *Foster their independence.* Don't feel guilty for not doing things for your parents that they could be doing for themselves. Instead, look for ways to help them do what they can. Something as simple as a $1.29 pill dispenser can help your parent be more independent—and can free up precious time for you.

9. *Face the facts.* Despite how much you want to help, sometimes your parent needs round-the-clock care and constant supervision that you *can't* provide. When that happens, acknowledge that someone (or some place) may be better equipped to provide the majority of your parent's care than you are.

10. *Don't succumb to peer pressure.* Acknowledge, but don't be unduly influenced by, the advice you get from friends and coworkers. Do what your heart tells you is best and what your circumstances permit.

Three

HOW CAN I GET FAMILY
MEMBERS TO HELP?

Do you feel like you're doing it all? Do you spend most of your time and energy caring for your parent while your siblings continue to take vacations, sleep late on weekends, and pursue personal interests? Are you sacrificing your own health and sanity to be a caregiver while your brother, sister, spouse, or other family members rarely lift a finger to help? Are you sick of going it alone?

Though you may feel alone in your own family, you're in good company. Millions of women across the country feel like you do. In one survey, 76 percent of family caregivers—most of them women—said they don't receive help from other family members. As exhausting as caregiving can be under any circumstances, it is even more tiring and frustrating if you're surrounded by family members who don't seem to want to help. In fact, many women say that dealing with unhelpful siblings is one of the most stressful aspects of caregiving.

Fortunately, being a caregiver doesn't have to be a one-person job, even in a family full of seemingly self-centered or reluctant individuals. It will take effort, ingenuity, and, at times, cold, hard cash, but in most cases, you can gain the cooperation of siblings and other family members and get the help you need. In this chapter, I'll offer specific strategies to help ensure that you won't have to go it alone.

Hold a Family Meeting

If your family is like most, you don't all live in the same city—or maybe not even within a day's drive of one another. You're here and there, with jobs, families, and responsibilities. Yet the decisions and responsibilities of caring for an elderly parent must sometimes be handled as a family. A good way to do that is with a family meeting.

The time to plan a family meeting is *before* your parent(s) has a crisis that requires immediate attention. Be proactive. Clues from your parent—such as increasing forgetfulness, missed medications, or difficulties managing money, keeping house, or getting to appointments—are all signs that a family meeting may be in order.

To plan a family meeting, think of everyone who is or should be involved in caregiving and caregiving decisions (siblings, spouses, and even your parents, if possible) and begin to consider arrangements for a time and meeting place. Ideally, you should meet with your family face-to-face. If that's not possible, a telephone conference call or even a private Web chat should suffice. And by the way, never end a meeting, call, or chat without scheduling your next meeting.

If you've had disagreements with your family over caregiving or if some family members are behaving emotionally or irrationally, it may be helpful to enlist the help of an objective third party, such as a counselor or social worker, particularly one who is experienced in geriatric case management. This person cannot only facilitate the meeting, he or she can also provide information about caregiving options that you and your family may not have considered or even be aware of. To find a geriatric case manager in your area, contact the National Association of Professional Geriatric Care Managers at (602) 881-8008 or call the Area Agency on Aging's Eldercare Locator at (800) 677-1116.

During your meeting, you can discuss major caregiving decisions (for example: Should Mother move in with a family member and, if so, which one? Should we check into assisted-living centers or nursing homes?) and divisions of responsibilities (Who will drive her to doctor's appointments? Who will pick up her medications? Who will handle her shopping and banking?). Be proactive—make decisions before they need to be made.

The following ten tips will help make your family meeting more efficient and productive.

1. **Meet ASAP.** If a crisis has happened and you are the primary caregiver, the sooner you hold the meeting, the sooner you can get help and the less time your family members have to get stuck in the comfortable rut of letting you do all the work.

2. **Set the agenda.** This meeting is serious business. Make up an agenda just as you would if you were holding a business meeting. Carefully consider which decisions need to be made and which tasks need to be completed. Write them all down in advance. If possible, mail, e-mail, or fax a copy to all family members before the meeting. This will give them time to consider how they can best help before they meet with the group. It will also save time and hassle once you get together and will help ensure that the most important issues are covered.

3. **Establish meeting rules.** One person should lead the meeting. Often, this is the person who is closest (either geographically and/or emotionally) to the parent and who will most likely be the primary caregiver. In some cases, people have a family friend or less involved third party lead the meeting. Make it clear that each person should treat the others with respect. No shouting. No interrupting. No name-calling. You get the idea.

4. **Give everyone time to talk.** Everyone should have the opportunity to provide input and have your full attention while they speak. To ensure that even quiet family members get a chance to talk, give each one an allotted time. You might want to call on them in alphabetical order or in order of age.

5. **Ask for volunteers.** Give everyone the opportunity to volunteer for particular tasks (such as locating legal documents, picking up your parent's prescriptions, or hiring a home health aide). Before the meeting, decide whom you would choose for each job and make a list. Consider your family members' talents and interests—which jobs would they do well? Which jobs would they most likely enjoy? If no one volunteers for tasks you can't do on your own, start recruiting based on your list.

6. **Be specific.** If you need help with certain caregiving tasks, be specific with your requests. For example, "Mom gets a senior discount at the grocery store on Wednesdays. Would one of you be able to take her to the grocery store each Wednesday morning?" or "I have to be out of town on business March 10 through 14. Could one of you plan to check on her daily and be on call for her those days?"

CREATING A CAREGIVERS' CALENDAR

When several family members are involved in a loved one's care, keeping up with who does what and when can be a challenge. That's why it's important to keep a master calendar that everyone involved in your parent's care has access to.

To create a master calendar, purchase a calendar that has plenty of room for writing. Go through the whole year, filling in any dates you know that you or a family member will be called on to help—for example, her long-standing appointment with her dentist or her weekly appointment with the physical therapist or hairdresser. Also, make a note of specific times that you plan or need to be off. If you don't have any plans to be off, make some. Pick a week or two during the year and mark that time on the calendar—you're going to need a break.

As various family members commit to handling specific caregiving duties, add their names to the calendar next to the time and duty. Then, each month, send a copy of the next month's calendar to each involved family member. Along with the month's calendar, include an overview of the months ahead: your vacation next June, during which your sister will be filling in for you for a week; your mother's college reunion in August, which your brother promised to take her to; and your father's Thanksgiving trip, for which your aunt promised to purchase airline tickets and arrange transportation to and from the airport.

You can send the calendars by mail, fax, or e-mail. Whichever way you choose to create and distribute your calendars, have family members confirm when they receive their calendar and call you if they have any questions about their commitment.

Let family members know that if they find they can't fulfill their duties, they *must* find someone else to take them. Ideally, they should seek the help of another family member. If other family members aren't available, they should look to friends for help or hire someone.

If you are your parent's primary caregiver, unfortunately, the task of creating and keeping up with the calendar will most likely fall on you. However, I think you will find the benefits of increased family cooperation well worth the hassle.

7. **Focus on the issue at hand.** Your sister was rude to you last Thanksgiving. Your brother's rowdy kids practically wrecked your home. Sure, you have grievances with your siblings, but now is not the time to bring them up or let them influence your decisions. The family meeting is to discuss your parent's care—nothing more. Stick to the task.

8. **Look to the future.** As you arrange your parent's care for the here and now, don't forget that health and abilities change—sometimes quickly. Come up with a contingency plan—or at least the agreement to hold another family meeting if your parent's condition changes and you need to make new arrangements or assign new responsibilities.

9. **Establish a spokesperson.** If your parent needs someone to communicate with his or her doctor and other health profes-

sionals, it's much better to assign one person to the task. Pick someone who is reliable, has good communication skills, and is willing to keep other family members up to date on your parent's health information. Often this will be the primary caregiver, because this person (often you) has the main responsibility for the parent's care and probably has the closest relationship with the medical team.

10. **Request a break.** If family members live far from your parent and have difficulty participating in day-to-day care, request that they devote one week of their vacation time each year to give you a break. If that's not possible, at least ask for an occasional weekend. Get them to commit to specific dates in writing. Depending on your parent's health, he or she may be able to travel to them or they may need to come to the parent. The important thing is that you get at least one complete week to relax and rejuvenate away from your parent.

Let Them Know You Need Them

Often caregivers become overburdened because they are victims of their own success. When family members see how well you handle the job, they may assume you don't need their help—so they simply don't offer.

If you have assumed the role of primary caregiver, it may well be that you are the best person to manage the job. But managing the job doesn't mean doing the whole job yourself. One quality of a good manager is the ability to delegate. You must learn to assign tasks and pull it all together—to work smarter, not harder, as they say in business.

Unless you ask, your siblings might think you don't need or want their help. You can't expect them to read your mind, and

62 · The Caregiver's Survival Handbook

dropping hints may only make you seem like a complainer. When requesting help from your siblings, be clear about what you need. For example, saying, "Mom has a dental appointment on Monday at 2 P.M.—could you take her?" is a lot more effective than saying, "I wish you would take her to her appointments sometimes. I don't know why I should always be the one to do it."

Rachel learned the importance of asking for help when her father fractured two vertebrae in his spine. "He was in a lot of pain and could barely get out of bed most days," she said. "I was doing everything for him, yet my sister, who lives just ten minutes away, didn't even offer to help."

When Rachel became exhausted and felt she had no choice but to ask for help, she was surprised how receptive her sister was. "I made a list of all I do for Dad in a typical day and a typical week. I had her take a look at it and tell me if there were some tasks she might help with," Rachel said. "I could hardly believe it when she suggested we divide the list evenly!"

Today, Rachel has a lot more time for herself and she's more rested and better able to care for her father. Her sister, who has stood by her commitment to split the caregiving tasks with Rachel, is glad Rachel asked her help. "She tells me she 'needed to feel needed,' " Rachel says.

Let Bygones Be Bygones

When siblings squabble over who will care for Mom or Dad or refuse to help one another with caregiving tasks, the problem often isn't about caregiving itself, but conflicts and power struggles that may have existed since childhood.

As I mentioned previously in this chapter, this is not the time to hold grudges or bring up old grievances with your siblings.

Maybe your sister never had to study as hard as you did, or maybe she stole your boyfriend while you were away at camp. Perhaps your brother was always your parents' favorite. While you worked to pay the insurance on your old Dodge Duster, your brother received a shiny new Firebird on his sixteenth birthday. Sure you're mad. Sure this hurt you. But try to put aside anger and hurt feelings for your parent's sake and your own sanity, and focus on the present. The task at hand is taking care of your parent and yourself.

Sherry and Karen, now forty-five and forty-seven, had competed against each other for as long as they could remember. As youth, the two girls were always vying for their parents' attention and affection, and were all too eager to tattle when the other did something wrong. In high school, Sherry was jealous when Karen was elected homecoming queen, while Sherry was teased for being a bookworm. In college, Karen sulked when her younger sister excelled, while she barely got by with Cs. As adults, Sherry thought her older sister was superficial; Karen thought Sherry was too serious. The two women argued over virtually everything until both of their parents became ill. They realized they had to set aside their differences if they were going to be effective caregivers.

With some heartfelt discussions and the help of a counselor, Karen and Sherry learned to use their differences to their advantage. Karen used her people skills to garner the help of family members and communicate with their parents' health-care professionals. Sherry used her practicality and intellect to manage her parents' finances and research and understand their medical problems. As a result, their parents got the care they needed, and the two sisters got along better than they ever had.

If you find that you simply can't coordinate caregiving with your siblings, consider family counseling, as Karen and Sherry did. A counselor may be able to help you resolve your differences or at least put them aside while you work together toward a common goal.

Look Beyond Your Siblings for Help

As Peggy's mother, Jean, approached eighty-five, Peggy wondered how much longer Jean could live alone in the big old farmhouse where Peggy grew up. Yet she knew she couldn't handle her mother living with her. Suffering from both osteoporosis and arthritis herself, Peggy relied on her husband for much of her own care; she certainly couldn't expect him to take on her mother too. Being an only child, she wondered, "Who will take care of Mom?"

Peggy thought she had no choice but to move her mother to an assisted-living home until her thirty-one-year-old daughter, Amanda, volunteered to help care for Grandma. Two months later, Amanda left her high-rise apartment in town to live with her grandmother thirty miles outside of town—and forty-five minutes from Amanda's job.

"At first I was concerned that Amanda didn't realize what she was getting herself into," Peggy said. "I thought being young and single, she wouldn't like living so far from town with her grandmother, but for now she seems happy. Mother appreciates having someone stay with her at night and to run errands or help with housework on weekends. Amanda loves being with her grandmother, plus she's saving a fortune in rent."

Amanda is part of a growing trend—grandchildren caring for their grandparents. As life expectancies increase, many people are living not only into old age but into their children's old age. A woman who lives into her eighties or nineties, for example, is likely to have children in their sixties or even seventies. Like

Peggy, many sixty-and seventy-year-olds have health problems of their own and simply aren't up to the rigors of caregiving. That's when grown grandchildren can help out. "Adult grandchildren, who usually have a special affection for their grandparents, are likely to be in better physical shape to provide care than their graying parents," says Terry Mills, a sociology professor at the University of Florida in Gainesville who has studied the relationship between grandparents and grown grandchildren.

In addition to grandchildren, caregivers may also be siblings, nieces, cousins, or other relatives or family friends. In other words, caregivers aren't always the older person's own children. In some communities, the term *fictive kin* is used to refer to family ties that are based on relationships other than genetic (or being a "blood relative"). It is common for children to be raised by "aunts" or the elderly to be cared for by family who are not genetically related.

In one study of 142 elderly women, more than 40 percent could identify a fictive family member. Moreover, most of the women who had a fictive family member said that person lived relatively close to them.

If you need help with caregiving or simply aren't able to be a caregiver yourself, feel free to look beyond your own siblings and "blood" relatives. Your parent's neighbors, longtime friends, or members of a place of worship are all good prospects. People don't have to be related by blood to have deep feelings of affection and responsibility toward one another.

Even if friends and neighbors don't take a major or formal role in caring for your parent, it's nice to know that responsible people who love your parent are nearby if needed.

A friend of mine says she'll always be grateful to a young family who lived across the street from her grandmother and "adopted" her. "The kids called her Grandma Helen and looked after her in little ways—getting her mail or shoveling her step," she says. "It was not necessarily major caregiving, but it really helped all of us to know she was safe and cared for."

Don't Discount Men

Do you constantly turn to your sister-in-law for help without even considering that your brother may be willing and able to help with your parent? Do you bypass your husband, brothers-in-law, sons, and nephews when it comes to caregiving requests? If so, you may have a wealth of untapped resources right at your fingertips.

Just because women make up the vast majority of caregivers doesn't mean that men can't be good caregivers too. In fact, statistics show that roughly 28 percent of American men are now serving as their parent's primary caregiver. As more women work outside the home, more men are accepting a greater responsibility for the care of their families. And many men are growing to truly value family relationships—including their relationship with their aging parents. The payoff of a son-parent relationship can be rich for all involved. Parents can enjoy the companionship of their sons, sons can gain the benefits of loving and caring for their parents, and the women of the family—who traditionally have been responsible for virtually everything—get a break!

One of the most touching caregiving stories I have heard was about a missionary who left his post in Zambia to care for his mother in the United States, who was suffering from osteoporosis-related bone fractures. At first, he planned to take care of her for only a short while, until her fractures healed. But just as one bone began to heal, it seemed another one would break. At the same time, his father suffered a series of strokes. In addition to caring for his mother, the man took the responsibility of bathing and dressing his father.

Although his father has since died, the missionary continues to care for his mother. What he thought would be a short trip back to the United States has now lasted for more than fifteen years, and he says he has never regretted his decision to come back and help his parents. As a matter of fact, he considers the time spent caring for his parents to be a gift.

Unlike the missionary, many male caregivers never volunteer for the job. Some men need a push to get them going in the right direction. Sarah's husband, Jim, is a good example. Sarah and Jim had been married just three years, and Sarah was newly pregnant with their first child when Jim's widowed father suffered a stroke. For a few months afterward, Sarah did all she could to help her father-in-law, while also attending graduate school and trying to take care of herself and their unborn baby.

But difficulties arose when Sarah realized that Jim *expected* her to take care of his father—after all, she was a woman and she wasn't earning an income, he told her. "Besides," he said, "taking care of my dad is good practice for when the baby comes."

Jim's attitude changed when Sarah had pregnancy complications and her doctor put her on strict bed rest for the last eight weeks of her pregnancy. Fearing the loss of his baby—and perhaps Sarah as well—Jim enforced the doctor's orders. He also got a taste of caregiving—for both his wife and father.

Though Sarah's mother came to help her out, the primary responsibility for Jim's father rested on Jim. To Sarah's surprise, Jim thrived in his caregiving role. He had to take time off from his job—which he had intended to save for their baby's first weeks—but otherwise he managed quite well. As Jim's father grew stronger, so did his relationship with his son.

Jim's father was fortunate. Less than six months after his stroke—and shortly before Jim and Sarah's baby girl was born—he was able to return to his own home with minimal assistance from Jim and Sarah.

"Jim's dad is doing well now, and he doesn't need Jim's help every day like he did," Sarah says. "But it's wonderful to see how caring Jim is now toward his dad and our little girl. I think he had it in him all along. I guess he just needed a push."

Jim's story is a perfect example of what a man can do if he is called upon. If you make a man step up to the plate, you may be surprised at how much of a help he can be, and he might just be surprised at how much *he* gets out of the relationship.

If you want to ask a man for help, you need to know how to approach him—butter him up, feed his ego. Make him feel that you are asking for his help because he is the only one you can fully trust with the job—even if you are desperate for any help you can get! Also, try to match your requests to his macho self-image. While your brother or husband will probably fume if you ask him to take your mother shopping or to the hair salon, he may not balk at checking out the squeak in her car, building a ramp to her front porch, fixing her leaky faucet, or installing a VCR so she can watch her soap opera tapes.

One important note: When he has finished the job—no matter how small—be sure to brag on him and thank him. That's the best way to ensure he'll help with a bigger project later!

Consider Talents and Interests

Your sister is an accountant, your brother is a chef, your sister-in-law is a great organizer, and your nephew loves nothing better than to drive his new car. Why not ask them to do what they do best? When you help match caregiving tasks to interests and abilities, you're more likely to get cooperation from all involved.

That's what Jane discovered. She was constantly asking her younger sister, Sue, if she would take their mother to her doctors' appointments. Even though Sue didn't work outside the home (she had a part-time scrapbooking business that she ran from her basement), she always seemed to come up with some reason she couldn't drive their mother.

Finally, Sue confided to her sister that she was afraid to drive in downtown traffic, and that getting her mother and her wheelchair in and out of the car was difficult for her. She said she would be glad to help in some other way. But how?

Jane thought hard about what her sister could and would be willing to do. "I decided what impressed me most about Sue was her ability to keep a spotless and well-organized home—so unlike mine."

Then Jane had an idea. Ever since her mother's arthritis had become so severe that she had to use a wheelchair most of the time to get around—even around the house—she had complained about not being able to reach the things she needed on shelves. Perhaps Sue might help her mother organize her home so that her most frequently needed items were at waist level or below. Sue was glad to help. She spent a couple of weeks with her mother, organizing items on shelves, in cabinets, and in drawers so that her mother could reach them more easily.

While she was organizing, she found a box of family photos going back to her childhood. She asked her mother if she could have them.

The following Christmas, Sue presented her mother with three lovely scrapbooks she had created from the photos her mother had given her. Her talents and interests had been useful not only in organizing her mother's home, but in organizing forty-five years of her family's history into a set of attractive books the family could enjoy for generations. Tapping in to Sue's interests and talents paid off for everyone.

When you seek out tasks that match people's talents, be thoughtful to consider what they enjoy doing as well as what they do for a living. But be careful; don't make assumptions that what they *like* to do is what they do professionally. Some people prefer to keep what they do for money and for family separate. For example, my friend Bob is a financial planner. When his wife's mother wanted some advice on investments that would help pay for long-term care, Bob referred her to a colleague. His mother-in-law seemed surprised and his wife acted like he was a jerk. "It wasn't that I didn't want to help her," Bob said, "but financial planning is my job—it's what strangers pay me to do. I didn't want to take responsibility for what my mother-in-law did with her money—kind of like a doctor doesn't want to treat members of his own family."

While Bob never offered his mother-in-law free financial advice, he did offer to help her fix up the home where she had spent the past forty years. Later, when she moved to a high-rise condo in town, Bob coordinated the packing and moving for her.

By carefully considering what various family members *can* do and *enjoy* doing and then matching jobs to both skills and interests, you're likely to get their much-needed help and cooperation.

Hold Your Criticism

When Grace's mother was diagnosed with congestive heart failure, no one else in the family could do anything to Grace's satisfaction. "If I tried to help by taking Mom a meal, Grace complained that I had used fat cuts of meat or that I had used canned vegetables instead of fresh," said her sister, Rebecca. "If I took Mom to the doctor's office, Grace asked why I had driven my van instead of borrowing my husband's sedan with the leather seats—the velour seats were hard for Mom to slide into. When our brother stopped by Mom's house one day after work to drop off a prescription and a pint of her favorite sherbet, Grace criticized him for not staying longer and helping Mom out—hadn't he noticed the chipping paint on Mom's shutters or that the faucet in the bathroom dripped? No matter what we did to try to help, Grace made us sorry."

Though Rebecca loved her mother and wanted to be with her, she grew weary of Grace's criticism. "I know it was wrong, but I gradually spent less and less time doing things for Mom. Of course, Grace noticed that too, and called to chew me out one day because she was bearing the burden of caring for Mom alone."

The story of Grace and Rebecca reminds me of the saying "No good deed goes unpunished." For all of their acts of kindness, Rebecca and her brother took a lot of punishment from their sister, who wanted to call all the shots in regard to their mother's care. No doubt they would have been much more willing to help if their sister had only heeded another saying my grandmother uses: "You can catch more flies with honey than with vinegar."

You'd be surprised how many stories I hear about caregivers who are critical of those who try to help them but then become angry and frustrated when those same people stop trying to help. These overly critical caregivers are often martyrs. Martyrs somehow feel they must handle every aspect of caregiving on their own, because no one else is capable enough or caring enough for the job. Instead of finding joy in caring for her parents, a martyr focuses on the sacrifices she is making. Her main source of satisfaction is the pity she evokes in others. Nothing boosts her self-esteem more than hearing someone say, "Poor woman, she's caring for her mother night and day with no help from the rest of the family."

If you find yourself becoming a martyr, stop it! Developing relationships and interests away from your parents can help boost your self-esteem and give you the energy to care with more joy and less concern about your sacrifices. Graciously accepting help with caregiving can give you time to care for yourself and to do things you enjoy.

Believe it or not, some caregivers criticize others as a way of keeping them away. Some women are jealous of the time a parent spends with another sibling. If you think you may be subconsciously trying to keep siblings away with your criticism, remember that your siblings have a right and responsibility to spend time with your parents and participate in their care.

On the other hand, if you're trying to gain the cooperation of siblings who either don't do enough or don't do things your way, you'll have a lot better luck with praise and thanks (honey) for steps in the right direction than by criticism (vinegar) of what you don't like.

Of course, there are times when being critical, scolding, or taking more aggressive action is warranted. Though it is rare, I do hear stories of caregivers who drive with their parents while drinking or who treat their parents very harshly. Also, we have all heard horror stories of caregivers who slap, verbally abuse, or neglect their elderly family members. By all means, if something like that is going on, you need to speak up. Anyone who continues to treat a family member this way should no longer be allowed to "care" for them. Likewise, if your siblings are not heeding your parent's dietary restrictions when preparing meals or are failing to give medications on time, you need to speak up. But if they simply have different ways of doing things from you, praise what you see as positive but let the rest slide.

Consider Caring Styles

You visit your mother twice a week. You fix her hair, hold her hand, sip coffee over the kitchen table with her, and listen lovingly and sympathetically as she describes her latest ailments. Your sister sends her flowers once a month, but rarely visits. Your brother visits occasionally, but when he does, he's more intent on mowing her lawn or fixing a leaky faucet or creaky floorboard. Who cares about your mother the most?

Though it probably feels like you are the most caring sibling, consider that the three of you may simply show love differently.

In the popular series of books, *The Five Love Languages,* author Gary Chapman explains that people express and receive love best through one of five different communication styles: quality time, words of affirmation, gifts, acts of service, and physical touch.

If you show your mother love through touch and spending time together, you probably feel most loved by people who touch and spend time with you. Perhaps you have even told your husband, "Don't worry about buying me a Valentine's Day present. Just be sweet to me all year."

Your sister, on the other hand, may see giving and receiving gifts as a way to show love. She's the type whose husband wouldn't dare come home without a Valentine's gift! Your brother, who expresses love by acts of service, could care less about Valentine's gifts or sweet talk—as long as his wife does the laundry and puts dinner on the table (acts of service).

Instead of seeing one of you as more caring than the others—

which can lead to competition, anger, and resentment—make the most of your caring styles. Ideally, all of us should be the recipients of our loved ones' touch, time, gifts, affirming words, and acts of service. But it's not necessary that we get them all from the same person.

If your sister continues to send flowers, for example, and your mother enjoys them, let them keep coming. On the other hand, if there are things your mother needs that your sister could provide, let her know. Maybe your sister sends flowers because she herself loves flowers, but she might be just as happy to send gifts of fresh fruit or even occasional checks to cover minor household expenses. Your brother's acts of service, though they may not seem loving to you, are helpful in keeping your mother's house in good repair. Count her lucky! What some of us wouldn't give for a good handyman now and then!

If Necessary, Resort to Bribes and Payment

Your mother needs a ride to the doctor. If you don't take her yourself, you'll need to pay taxi fare or have a service pick her up. But wouldn't she rather ride with your sister than a stranger? If your sibling isn't willing or able to take time for your mother simply out of love or sheer responsibility, she may well do it for cold, hard cash. It may sound mercenary, but as long as your mother gets the ride she needs and the company she craves and you get a break, there's probably no harm in making a financial arrangement with a sibling.

It worked for Shelia. A pharmaceutical sales rep who often travels for her job, Shelia was finding it increasingly difficult to schedule her mother's doctors' appointments and errands around her own travels. Though she had a younger sister in

✍ Make a Chore Jar

If friends or family members offer to help your parent, take them up on their offer. Even someone who stops by your mother's house for just an hour can help wash a load of dishes, replace a burned-out light in her bathroom, or make a pitcher of iced tea. For a fun way to assign tasks to visitors, create a chore jar, or maybe two of them. One could be labeled "quick chores"; the other could be labeled "bigger chores." Cut a bunch of strips of paper and keep them near the jars. When your parent needs something done, have her write it on a slip of paper and place it in the appropriate jar (or write it for her). For example, "loosen child-proof caps on my medicine bottles," "help me write a note to Aunt Betty," or "move the dishes in the cabinet over my oven to a lower, easier-to-reach shelf" would go in the "quick chores" jar. "Replace the cracked pane in my bedroom window" or "prune the shrubs" would go into the "bigger chores" jar. When visitors arrive—depending on the anticipated length of their visit—they can draw a chore from the jar and do it.

For a parent who is hesitant to ask for help, the chore jar eliminates the need to request help directly. Visitors can have fun reaching into the jar to see what their chore will be. It goes without saying that not every visitor should feel obligated to draw from the chore jar or that those who choose to should feel obligated to do the chore they select. If your petite twelve-year-old, for example, draws a slip that says "Replace rotten siding next to back door," let her know it's perfectly acceptable to return that slip to the jar and try again!

76 · The Caregiver's Survival Handbook

town who was perfectly capable of doing these tasks, her sister, Samantha, stayed busy with her job at a fast-food restaurant—a job she didn't enjoy, but one that was necessary to help support her family. If she took time off to help her mother, of course, she didn't get paid.

For Shelia, time was the issue; for Samantha, the issue was money, so the two made a deal. Samantha was able to cut back her hours at the restaurant and, each week, Shelia sent her sister a check for the difference in pay. Samantha used the extra time to help her mother with shopping, light housework, errands, and doctor's appointments.

Shelia was grateful to have someone she knew and trusted helping her mother, Samantha appreciated the break from her restaurant job and the opportunity to help her mother, and their mother got the care she needed and the companionship of her younger daughter. In other words, all three women won in this arrangement.

If you decide to pay a sibling to care for your parent, make sure they know what you expect of them just as you would if you were hiring a stranger. Be clear that you are paying them for a service, not giving them a handout. Finally, think twice before telling your parent about the financial arrangement with your sibling. As long as your parent gets the care she needs, she doesn't need to know that money is changing hands. (For more information on hiring relatives to care for a loved one, see Chapter 6.)

Know When to Say When

Sure you want your family to help, and they *should* help. But some people just won't and don't, and there's nothing you can do to change them. If you have tried everything you can to get a family member to help, let it go. Stop focusing on the problem and start looking for a solution. Being overly concerned about what others aren't doing and allowing yourself to become angry or sulk can affect your ability to be a good caregiver.

That's what Barb, a freelance graphic designer and single mother of a teenage son, discovered. After her mother fell and broke her hip, Barb was with her all the way, waiting at the hospital during surgery to repair the fractured hip, sitting by her bedside while she recuperated in the hospital, and, later, moving her mother into her home and helping with her care and rehabilitation.

At the same time, Barb's sister, who lived just an hour away, did virtually nothing. "She visited Mom at the hospital only once and called a few times to check on her, but essentially I was on my own," Barb said. "I thought once we got home, surely she would offer to help, but she didn't. In fact, she thought of every reason *not* to help me."

"On several occasions, I called her in tears, asking her if she could give me a break or help with Mom while I caught up on some of my work," Barb said. "But she always had some excuse—she couldn't take time off work, she had a dental appointment, her daughter was in a soccer tournament, or her husband had the flu and she hated to leave him. All the time I was fussing and fuming that I didn't get any help."

Although Barb was understandably angry and disappointed with her sister, she soon resolved not to call and ask for her help again. "If she calls me and wants to help Mom, I'll accept—gladly," she said. "But in the meantime I'm not forcing the issue. And I'm not wasting this precious time with my mother worrying about what someone else *isn't* doing."

While a sibling who won't help may be behaving like a selfish jerk, be careful not to judge. There may be reasons for their behavior that you don't understand. One woman told me her brothers couldn't understand why she didn't rush to her father's bedside when he had a heart attack. "They didn't know—I never told a soul—that in private my father had been verbally abusive toward me most of my life. Instead of being sad when my dad was sick, I secretly thought, 'It's payback time.' "

Others who don't help with their aging parents as much as their siblings think they should may have different, but equally legitimate, reasons. One man told me he wanted desperately to be with his elderly mother but had already used up all of his sick and annual leave from work and, moreover, he had his own family to support. "I was torn between being with my mother and providing for my family, but my sisters didn't seem to understand," he said.

If you have a sibling who refuses to help, maybe he or she has a reason or circumstances you are unaware of. Don't make a rash judgment but, better yet, give the benefit of the doubt. Try to talk to siblings about their reluctance to help. Ask if there are problems they would like to talk about or if there is anything you can do to help *them*. You may gain some insight; you may not. But always leave the door open for future conversations.

In the meantime, do what *you* know is right. As long as you do what's right by your parents, you won't have regrets. Your errant siblings, on the other hand, will have to live with themselves.

Turn to Professionals

If you are an only child or if, despite your best efforts, you can't get your family members to help with caregiving, you may need to turn to professionals. Fortunately, there are people capable of helping with virtually any task (including driving, bathing, dressing, grooming, cooking, housekeeping, changing bandages or catheters, administering medications, and running errands) your loved one might need. In fact, there are some tasks, such as bathing and dressing, both you and your parent might prefer that a professional handle.

If you work during the day or if you just need a break, adult day care centers offer daytime care and activities for seniors who are mobile. Many centers offer two-, three-, or five-day programs. Most even offer transportation. To find adult day care in your area, ask for referrals from your parent's doctor and other health professionals, check the Yellow Pages under Adult Day Care, or check out the following Web sites: www.nadsa.org (National Adult Day Services Association), www.aoa.gov (Administration of Aging), and www.caregiving-solutions.com (Caregiving Solutions).

If the cost of daytime care is prohibitive or if you're not near an adult day care center, research other options. One of the best ways to do that is to ask other people in your situation what they have done. One woman told me that she hired a nanny to take care of both her seventy-nine-year-old mother and her school-aged children. The nanny helps the woman's mother with bathing, dressing, and meal preparation in the morning and then meets her children at the school bus and helps with their homework while her mother naps in the afternoon. Another woman told me she and a friend chipped in to hire one full-time caregiver for both of their mothers. Both women work part-time and are usually able to arrange their schedules to work different shifts. The caregiver was willing to accept the arrangement because she was guaranteed a forty-hour workweek by splitting her time between the two families. All of these women found solutions to their caregiving needs by being creative and thinking outside of the box. If you are flexible, creative, and open to new ideas, chances are you'll find a caregiving solution that works for you.

Sometimes a change in job—or salary—is all you need to afford in-home care. For example, a woman I met at a seminar said that after struggling with the costs of caregiving, she finally had to tell her boss she would be unable to continue working because her salary barely covered the cost of her mother's care. Not surprisingly, her boss wanted to keep her on staff so badly that he gave her a considerable raise.

If you ever decide to approach your employer about your financial situation, first understand that you may need to look for a job the next day. That's what happened to another woman I met. When she told her boss she couldn't afford to pay for adult day care on her salary, he told her, "We will miss you, but we run a business, not a Welfare office."

Although the cost of care—both in-home and at adult day care centers—can be high, you can probably find alternate ways to afford it, if need be. Medicare, Medicaid, or long-term care policies cover some programs. To learn more about what these government programs offer in your state, check out www.caregivers.com or www.medicare.gov. There, you will find links or ways to search for information on your state's Medicaid and Medicare programs. Some centers operate on a sliding-fee scale. If cost is still an issue, ask if a sibling or other family member who is unable or unwilling to provide hands-on care will help foot the bill.

Even if you don't need help with the physical aspects of care right now, no doubt you could benefit from some emotional support yourself. Professionals, such as counselors, psychologists, or social workers, can help you cope with the emotional aspects of caring—particularly if you are going it alone. Some professionals facilitate support groups for caregivers, where you can meet and talk with others in similar situations.

If you are unable to attend support groups and you have access to a computer, there are many ways to seek support quickly and easily online—and you can even do so anonymously, if you prefer.

For support on the Internet, check out the following:

Chat Groups

Chat with others in real time via computer. Share your thoughts, feelings, and concerns; ask questions; and offer support. Like face-to-face support groups, chat groups are often scheduled for a particular time each week, though some meet more or less frequently. For a couple of chat groups you might want to visit, check out Virtual Carer support at www.zarcrom.com/users/yeartorem/candidchat.html or Eldercare online at www.ec-online.net.

Discussion Groups

Discussion groups offer the opportunity to send and receive information on particular topics by e-mail. To check out discussion groups, log on to Psychologist Online at www.psychologist-online.com or Today's Caregiver magazine at www.caregiver.com.

Message Boards

Have something you just have to get off your chest—right now? On a message board you can leave any message you wish at any time of day or night. Others logging on have the opportunity to read your message and respond. If you'd like to try out a message board, log on to www.SupportPath.com. The site offers an alphabetical listing of topics for message boards, chats, organizations, and information.

Be a Better Communicator

When it comes to coordinating a loved one's care and enlisting the help of family, good communication is key. By communication, I don't mean just the ability to speak calmly and clearly and relay information accurately (though these certainly are important aspects of good communication). Sometimes the most important skills of a good communicator are the abilities to sense when others are having problems, to ask questions tactfully, and then to be a patient and sympathetic listener.

Unfortunately, breakdowns in communication can occur just when we need to efficiently communicate most. A woman named Eva told me she was hurt when her sister criticized her for not helping out more after their mother's heart attack. "I really wanted to help more," Eva told me, "but I was going through my own medical crisis—I had just been diagnosed with breast cancer." Eva had kept her diagnosis a secret from her family, not wanting to upset her mother while she recovered from her heart attack.

Although Eva probably should have told her sister (if not her mother) what was going on in her own life, her sister also should have asked. If Eva's sister had been more sensitive toward her and gently asked why she wasn't helping instead of attacking her for not helping, the two sisters could have opened an important line of communication and been spared both anger and hurt feelings. And certainly Eva would have been eager to help her mother once she was physically and emotionally able.

We've addressed the topic of communication several times throughout this chapter, but that's because it so important . . . and so easy to mess up. If poor communication has become a problem in your family, remembering the following tips should help.

Speak to Each Other Directly

Remember the old game of gossip? The person at the head of the line comes up with a phrase and says it to the person next to her, who relays it to the next person and so forth until the last person in line repeats the phrase she heard. In the game, it was funny to hear how much the final message differed from the original. When communicating about caregiving, however, incorrect or misinterpreted information is no laughing matter. If you want someone to get your message—and get it right—speak to her directly instead of sending it down the grapevine. If you need to give the same message to several people and you don't relish the thought of repeating it, schedule a conference call, write it down and photocopy it, or send an e-mail message.

Be Specific

The more specific you can be about what you need a family member to do, the greater the chance they'll actually do it. General phrases like, "Can you try to help me out once in a while?" rarely bring the results you need. You'll probably be more successful with something like, "I'm going out of town for a wedding the week of June 23. Dad has physical therapy appointments on Tuesday and Thursday at 1 P.M. that week. Could you please take him one or both of those days?"

Speak Positively

If you speak negatively and critically, your family members might just tune you out. If you want their help, speak positively about what they have done and can do rather than negatively about what they can't or haven't done. A little positive reinforcement can work wonders. To use my mother's favorite expression, "Kill them with kindness."

Appoint a Spokesperson

When it comes to speaking with doctors and other health professionals, assign one person for the job. If you don't like repeating information to numerous family members, just think how your parent's doctor feels. By appointing a single spokesperson, you give your doctor one name to remember and one person to release information to regarding your parent's condition and care. Make sure the person you appoint has at least a rudimentary understanding of medical information and is willing and able to adequately relay that information to other family members.

Listen Patiently

You may not agree with everything your family members have to say, but give them a chance to speak—and truly listen. That way, each member feels as if his or her opinion is valued—which goes a long way toward gaining cooperation—and you just might learn something helpful.

Focus on the Issue

When discussing your parent's care, keep the conversation—and your mind, if possible—on the subject. Bringing up past grievances with your siblings, or allowing yourself to think of hurt feelings or broken promises, distracts you from what you're trying to do now.

Caring for an elderly parent is hard work, and you can't and shouldn't go it alone. When you need help, use communication, flattery, gimmicks (like the chore jar), bribes, or whatever necessary to get it. You and your parent deserve nothing less.

⅜ Ten Ways to Get Your Family to Help ⅜

1. *Let them know you need them.* Many times, family members would be happy to help if they knew their help was needed, so ask. Let your family know you need their help and, when possible, be specific about the help you need.

2. *Hold a family meeting.* Think of everyone who needs to be involved in caregiving (e.g. siblings, nieces, nephews, and spouses) and arrange a time and place to get together to discuss your loved one's care.

3. *Consider caring styles.* Just because your siblings care for your parent *differently* than you do, don't assume they don't care at all or stress out over who cares more. Be grateful for their caring gestures and take what you can get.

4. *Don't discount men.* When looking for help with caregiving, don't limit your search to the females in your family. Men are often willing and able to help out if you just ask.

5. *Hold your criticism.* No one will ever do everything completely to your liking, but that doesn't mean they don't care and can't help. Unless your siblings are endangering your parent's

life or well-being, holding your criticism is essential to gaining their cooperation.

6. *Consider talents and interests.* When you match caregiving jobs to your family's talents and interests, you're likely to get more cooperation.

7. *Look beyond siblings.* If you're an only child or if your sibling(s) simply aren't able or willing to help, look elsewhere; your parent's nieces, nephews, younger siblings, or grandchildren are all good choices for helping with caregiving tasks.

8. *Consider finances.* If a sibling has more money than time to offer your parent, ask her to pay for some of the services that you would otherwise have to do yourself.

9. *Show them the money.* Though it sounds mercenary, it may take cold, hard cash to get some family members to help out with your parent. Your parent never needs to know that your siblings are being paid for their services.

10. *Consider their circumstances.* If your sibling's failure to help with a parent's care is uncharacteristic behavior, instead of scolding him or her, try having a heart-to-heart about any problems he or she is facing. It just might start a healing process for both of you.

Four

HOW CAN I AVOID BUTTING HEADS WITH MY PARENT?

Does it ever seem that you and your parent can't agree on anything? Is your parent critical? Does your mother try to make you feel guilty when you don't do everything her way? Does your father clearly favor one of your siblings over you, when you are the one who takes care of him every day?

If you answered yes to any—or perhaps all—of these questions, you're not alone. I can't count the number of women who have told me that their relationship with their aging parent is fraught with conflict and hurt feelings. And no wonder. We all have issues from our childhood, personality conflicts, and unresolved problems. Why should it be any different for you and your parents now that you're older?

In fact, there's good reason to expect *more* conflict between you and your aging parent as you become a caregiver. The average family caregiver spends eighteen hours a week tending to a parent or older adult. In the most severe caregiving cases, when the person under her care lives in her home and has dementia, that figure increases to about eighty-seven hours of caregiving a week. That's a lot of togetherness, even in ideal circumstances.

But the circumstances under which we assume the caregiving role are usually far from optimal. The role changes that occur when you assume responsibility for your parent are difficult for all involved. For parents, accepting the losses and limitations of aging and facing their own mortality isn't easy. For children, it can be both upsetting and frightening to see the people who once took care of them unable to care for themselves. When a parent and child, each having to deal with his or her own issues, are forced into the new roles neither asked for, the setting is ripe for conflict.

Furthermore, few of us enter the caregiving role free of hurt feelings or areas of disagreement. There is at least some friction in virtually all parent-child relationships almost from the time we are born. When you were a toddler and threw a tantrum because your father wouldn't buy you candy, that was conflict. When you were fifteen and your mother didn't allow you to date even though all of your friends were doing it, that was conflict. Now that you've grown up, you may think the conflicts have been resolved—and many of them probably have. But whether you are aware of it or not, there are still likely to be some areas of unresolved differences, even as new differences and conflicts arise.

It has been said that whatever personality traits people have when they are young will only be magnified as they grow older. A woman who's fastidious about her housekeeping when she's young, for example, may become more so as she ages. A man who has a short fuse when his children are young may be even quicker to anger when they are grown. The same holds true of relationships as we age. Problems that are present in relationships when we are young don't just go away because we have grown up. In fact, unless we work to resolve them, they only become magnified and cause more trouble throughout the years.

In addition, the stresses of growing old and the losses that accompany old age and illness can cause unexpected changes in your loved one's personality. An otherwise mild-mannered parent may start to snap at you or criticize you. A parent who appreciated your every gesture of kindness several years ago may now respond angrily, instead of gratefully, when you try to help. A father who once seemed unflustered by just about anything may be quick tempered or become frustrated when his checkbook doesn't balance or he can't climb the steps like he used to.

Caregivers' personalities can change unexpectedly too. When plagued by an overwhelming sense of duty, lack of sleep, and sheer exhaustion, even the most patient and loving caregiver can find herself behaving in ways she never imagined.

Despite all that may be going against a harmonious relationship, there are ways to resolve conflicts so that your parent gets what is truly needed and your final years, months, or days together aren't full of fighting and hurt feelings. Dealing with an aging parent, as with anyone, requires give and take. Sometimes you have to compromise.

The situations that cause problems are as varied as the people and relationships are themselves, but there are several common—some almost universal—uncomfortable situations that caregivers must face. In the following pages, I discuss some of those challenges and offer suggestions for solving them with minimal head-butting and hurt feelings.

Why Is What I Do Never Enough for My Parent?

You make every effort to care for your parent. But instead of acting grateful for all you do, you get grief for what you *don't* do. Sound familiar?

The scenario was all too familiar to DeeDee, a friend of mine who, despite a full-time job and college classes two nights a week, spends a good part of each week with her aging parents. Regardless of how often she is with them or how long she stays when she visits, the response is the same from her parents when it's time for her to leave. "Why are you in such a hurry to go?" her father asks. "What's more important than your parents?" her mother chimes in.

"They're always doing that to me, and I hate it," DeeDee says. "I almost want to say, 'If you can't appreciate the time I do spend with you, maybe I just shouldn't come at all.'"

Many women tell me they are greeted by their parents with "Hello, stranger" or "It's about time you came to see your old man," even if they visited just a few days before. Others tell me that their parents don't seem to enjoy the time they are together because they are so concerned about the time they *aren't* together. When it comes time to end the visit, many women—like DeeDee—can't get away without insinuations that they would stay longer if they really cared.

If your parent's remarks make you feel like screaming or just stopping your visits altogether, avoid making any rash decisions. First consider the reasons he or she may be acting that way.

• *The need for reassurance.* At a time in their lives characterized by loss—of their friends and loved ones, health, abilities, and so forth—your parents may be scared that they will lose you too. Assure them that you still love them and will be there when they need you.

• *Jealousy.* Although it's hard to think of parents being jealous of their children, it happens. Your have your health, your family, your job, your life, your independence, and probably many opportunities they never had. They see any or all of these things as competition for your interest and affection. If you really loved them, they reason, you'd put them before the other interests in your life.

• *Difference of perspective.* For DeeDee, like many caregivers with jobs and other commitments, devoting even a few hours to caring for aging parents is difficult. A few hours in the evening seems like a long time when you have worked all day and you have more work—and possibly a family deserving of your attention—waiting for you when you get home. On the other hand, for the elderly parent with few responsibilities at this time in life and few interests except for a grown child, a few hours seems insignificant compared to the long, tedious hours they're alone. Seeing you provides a respite from boredom and loneliness. No wonder they don't want you to leave. And they're likely to resort to guilt tactics to keep you there longer and make you feel like you need to come back sooner.

• *Forgetfulness.* If your parent is cognitively impaired, perhaps he or she doesn't remember that you visited just yesterday or that you have been sitting on the sofa together for three hours. One woman told me she had been visiting her father with Alzheimer's when she excused herself to use the rest room. When she returned to the living room where he sat waiting, her father looked at her with exasperation. "I thought you'd be here hours ago," he snapped. "Was the traffic bad again?" Rather than argue that she had been with her father most of the day and had left the room for just a moment, she told him, "The traffic is always bad this time of day. I'm so glad I finally got to see you. I have missed you."

If a cognitively impaired parent argues that you are late or haven't visited, there is no reason to start a fight by telling him just how often or how long you do visit. Nor is there reason to feel guilty if your parent insinuates that you don't care if you don't spend enough time with her. You can gently tell her that you do love being with her but that the need to earn a living or care for your own home or family makes it impossible to spend as much time with her as you would like. Reassure her that you are always nearby, and in the event of an emergency, you will do all you can to get to her as quickly as possible.

Of course, even if your aging parent still has all his or her faculties, he or she will most likely want more time and attention than you can offer. One solution is to help your parent find other interests besides you. Having other places to direct attention will help relieve boredom. Encourage other family members and friends to visit your mother or take her out if she's able. Check into adult day care programs or programs at a nearby senior center. If your parent attends a place of worship, find out if they offer programs and activities for seniors.

One woman told me that her mother's church regularly took seniors on short day-trips or overnight trips to museums, plays, parks, nice restaurants, and other places of interest. Her mother complained that she would love to go on the trips, if only she could afford them. The daughter called the church's office and inquired about payment for the trip. She was able to arrange a deal with the seniors' director. She paid for the trip by credit card, which allowed the payments to be spread out, and as a bonus she received a gift certificate for one free trip!

Simple cards and gifts can be a good way to reassure an older relative who fears abandonment. A gift such as a large-print book, a videotape (if she has and can operate a VCR), a craft kit, or a gift certificate for her favorite store or restaurant will serve double-duty. She'll have the pleasure of opening the gift and knowing you're thinking of her, and she'll also have an activity to look forward to or something to keep her busy.

If you decide to try gift-giving, be careful. You don't want your parent to constantly expect gifts or planned activities. Nor do you want gifts and activities to replace the time you spend with her. Even so, a few dollars and an hour or so of planning now and then—when combined with your own reassurance— can let her know you care, improve her mood, and perhaps help reduce the number of times you have to hear, "It's about time you came for a visit" or "Why are you in such a hurry to leave?"

How Can I Get My Aging Parent to Stop Driving?

At first Claire's mother's accidents weren't so bad—backing into a shopping cart return at the supermarket, running over a curb and puncturing her front passenger-side tire, and hitting a friend's mailbox when pulling out of her driveway. But when the older woman came home with the front driver's-side fender bent so severely that it scraped against the tire—and then couldn't remember how it had gotten that way—Claire knew she had to intervene. "Scrapes and dents are one thing, but what if she has a serious accident that hurts her or someone else? I couldn't let that happen, yet I didn't know how to tell her."

Claire faced a difficult decision that many adult children and caretakers of older parents eventually face—getting a person who can no longer drive safely off the road. As people age, their vision, judgment, depth perception, and reaction time are impaired, which affects their ability to drive. Memory problems can make the situation even worse. One woman told me that she had given her mother a cell phone to use in the event she had car trouble or was lost. Often, her mother called from a mile or two away, asking for directions to get home. But one day she called ninety miles from her destination, saying she had mistakenly gotten on the interstate and didn't know how to get off. That's when the woman realized her mother shouldn't be driving.

Certainly, some older adults understand the time has come to stop driving and give up their keys agreeably, if not sadly. But in other cases, you'd have better luck taking the keys from a sixteen-year-old who just got a license!

For an older person (just as the teenager), a car represents independence and autonomy. At a time when their bodies may be failing them, their car still gets them where they want to go—and when they want to get there. Understandably, many people won't give that up without a fight. Would you?

Even if you are your parent's primary caretaker, you may not have to be the one to start that fight. Finding ways to enlist others can keep you from being the bad guy—or rather, girl!

Claire began by speaking with the eye doctor her mother had seen and trusted for the past twenty years. At her mother's next appointment, the doctor checked her eyes and reflexes and suggested she not be driving anymore. He told her gently he was required to write to the Department of Motor Vehicles (DMV) to have her license canceled.

Though Claire's mother was understandably upset—and Claire's caregiving duties increased since she now had to help her mother with transportation—she was never upset with Claire because her license had been taken away. Claire avoided being the villain, and was able to remain the sympathetic and concerned daughter her mother had always known.

Of course, you may prefer to speak directly with your parent and not get a doctor involved unless absolutely necessary. If you are really concerned that your parent's driving is putting him or her in danger, say so. Express your love and concern. Let your parent know you will be available as much as possible to help with transportation. Also, check out other sources of transportation that are available. Think of family members, friends, or neighbors who might drive your parent out of kindness or for money. Check the Yellow Pages under "transportation services." Check public transportation routes and schedules. For years, my grandmother got to town and was able to run many of her errands by taking a cab that stopped right outside her apartment.

Try to stay calm when speaking with your parent about his or her driving—he or she may be more receptive than you expect. When Marlene finally got up the nerve to tell her elderly mother that she thought it was time for her to give up driving, her mother wasn't as upset as Marlene had expected. "In fact, she seemed relieved," Marlene said. "She told me that she too had been concerned about her driving. She said she had been wanting to tell me for a while, but that she didn't want to burden me."

While changes in driving ability are usually gradual and give you time to deal with this issue carefully, there are definitely exceptions. If your parent's driving presents a personal or outside danger, or if he or she refuses to stop driving despite his doctor's recommendation, you may need to call the DMV directly and explain the situation.

If despite a doctor's recommendation and DMV orders your parent still insists on driving, simply take away the keys. If you do, put them where you parent can't find them and make sure there aren't copies hidden somewhere. If you suspect he or she has copies, put a device on the steering wheel that keeps the car from operating.

For some older people, just keeping the car in their driveway and their car keys in their purse or pocket can give them a sense of comfort—even if they know they will never be able to drive. If you are certain your parent won't venture out (and you can handle the cost of keeping the car), there's probably no harm in keeping it around. If you have any doubts as to whether your parent will actually try to use those keys, take them to a hardware store and have an extra notch added to them. They will still be the car keys he or she has always had, but they won't start the car.

How Can I Discuss the Possibility of Selling My Parents' Home?

For many seniors, nothing strikes "home" the fact that times are changing like, well, having to leave their home. For people who have lived in the same home for a long time, especially if they raised their children there, selling their family home may be particularly difficult. But for some, a move to an apartment, senior community, or assisted-living center promises a welcome new way of life—one free of climbing steps, mowing lawns, raking leaves, repairing fences, shoveling snow, and cleaning gutters (or, in the case of the latter, having to hire and pay someone to do those things). In those situations, the adult children may be more upset by the move than the parents.

If your parents are initiating a move and you are upset, try to understand it's probably in their best interest. If they want or need help, offer to assist in getting their home ready to sell, selecting new living arrangements, finding the best financing, and moving their possessions. If it helps you, spend time reminiscing with them about their home and all that happened there—especially if it's the home where you grew up. Ask if you can select some special items that will remind you of the house—perhaps a picture that used to hang on your bedroom wall or a pretty vase that always held cut flowers on your mother's dining room table. If you have the space in your home, maybe you would like larger items such as the dining room table itself. Also be sure they are able to locate and keep items that are important to them to help their new living space feel comfortable.

If it's your parents who are resisting the move, play up the positives of leaving a home they may no longer be able to manage—for example, no leaves to rake in the fall or snow-covered driveways to clear in the winter. If they are moving from their own home to an apartment, many of the hassles of home ownership—clogged gutters, leaky faucets, burst pipes, rotten floorboards, and broken air conditioners—become the responsibility of their landlord. With fewer hassles, they'll have more time to do the things they enjoy.

Also, help your parents find new living arrangements that will suit them. Though finances and their level of independence may limit the options, you probably have more choices than you realize. Remember, always be creative. One woman told me that when her parents became unable to care for the two-story home where she grew up, neither she nor they felt they could be happy anywhere else. After looking at more than a dozen senior communities, she and her husband came up with a plan. They moved into the house themselves and had the basement finished into a walk-in level apartment for her parents. "It turned out to be the perfect solution," she said. "My parents didn't have to sell the house, they still have their own space, and I'm close by in case they need me."

How Can I Get My Parents to Accept Help with Chores?

When Cindy visited her family for the holidays, the mess she found shocked her. The furniture was covered in thick dust, the kitchen counter was stacked high with dirty dishes, the refrigerator was full of moldy food, and the bathroom smelled like an outhouse.

Living out of state, there was little Cindy could do herself to keep up with her parents' home, but it was obvious they needed help, so Cindy quickly got to work looking for a part-time housekeeper. After three weeks of interviewing and checking references, Cindy found someone whom she considered to be the perfect candidate. Everything was set—or so she thought. When the woman showed up at her parents' home, Cindy's father wouldn't let her through the front door.

When Cindy learned what had happened, she was furious. "How could you?" she asked her father. "Do you enjoy living in filth? I can't help you if you won't let me."

Cindy's anger was understandable; her situation was not unusual. While many older people welcome the help and company of paid housekeepers, many others see housekeepers—or any other nonfamily helpers—as intruders.

Raised at a time when housework was "family" work and money may not have been plentiful, some seniors consider hiring a housekeeper to be frivolous. Others see getting outside help as admitting they can no longer take care of their own home. For a woman who always prided herself on her ability to keep a spotless home, that can be a difficult admission.

Still other seniors simply don't like the thought of having strangers in their home. They may fear invasion of their privacy or theft of money or belongings. They may even fear for their own safety.

If your parent refuses any kind of in-home help, try to find out why. The answer can help you find the solution. When Cindy spoke with her parents, she learned that her father was embarrassed for a stranger to see how dirty their house was, so Cindy came up with a plan. She called back the woman and asked if she would return the following week. In the meantime, she and her two teenagers flew to her parents' for the weekend and spent two days of intense cleaning. "It seemed kind of crazy to clean up for the cleaning lady," Cindy recalled, laughing, "but it helped."

When the maid returned the following week, Cindy's father wasn't ashamed to let her in. The house was in pretty good shape, and since the maid came every week after that, the house never returned to the state it was in when she first attempted to clean it. Cindy's parents decided they enjoyed having a clean house enough to put up with the slight discomfort of having a stranger in their home. Cindy's mother was glad she no longer had to struggle with the cleaning. And best of all: Once they were no longer ashamed of their home, Cindy's parents were willing to more readily open their home to friends and relatives.

If your parents fear for their possessions and safety, those fears can be alleviated as well. Go through an agency that bonds all of its employees. Ask for references of anyone they recommend. Get your parents a small safe, if they don't have one. It may comfort them to lock up cash, jewelry, medications (particularly pain killers, if they take them), and other valuables before the housekeeper arrives. Another option: Ask if they would like to give you some items for safekeeping.

If your parents still refuse help and you feel their dirty house is a health hazard, you may need to take more drastic action. Instead of cleaning it up yourself, some experts recommend calling Adult Protective Services (APS) and asking them to drop by your parents' house for a "routine" check. You can then request that APS inform your parents that their home must be cleaned for health reasons. This is *extreme*, so make sure the action is warranted.

When your parents share the news of the APS visit and that their home has to be cleaned, you can appear to be the supportive, helpful daughter who finds someone to clean their home.

How Can I Get My Parents to Let Me Help with Their Finances?

If you act too interested in your parents' finances, they may get uneasy. But it's never too early to find out what you can—particularly if you expect to have to support one or both of your parents in the future. The best time to start talking finances is when your parents still appear to be managing them pretty well. Bring up the subject by telling them that you need some key financial information—such as income, assets, expenses, and the locations of financial papers and their safe deposit box—so that you can help them if you ever need to. Also, be sure that you are a co-signer so that you can access the safe deposit box or write checks at a later date, if necessary.

If your parents fight you, ask them to reconsider giving you the information, especially if they appear to be having financial troubles. If they still don't budge, ask once more at a later date—when both you and your parents are relaxed. Don't get upset or insist that they give you the information. Just let them know you're available to help when and if they need you.

As Christine's parents reached their mid-seventies, she asked several times about their finances—with little luck. "They said they could manage their own money, thank you, and would let me know if they needed my help," she said.

About five years later, when Christine's mother ran up a $5,000 tab with a cable shopping channel and her parents' electricity was turned off because her father had repeatedly forgotten to pay the electric bill, Christine's father called her. She was able to get their electric service restored, return many of her mother's TV purchases and get their finances back on track. She worked with them to develop a budget they could stick with and then helped them twice a month with their bills.

Some older people, like Christine's parents, will seek financial help when they need it; others may keep financial troubles to themselves, either out of embarrassment or hesitation to give up control of their money.

If your parents' medical bills start to mount, if creditors call, or if their house is filled with frivolous purchases while their bills remain unpaid, you'll need to intervene—whether they ask you to or not. At that point, your parents may be secretly relieved that you have taken charge. In fact, you may face more opposition from siblings or other family members—who believe they should be the ones handling your parents finances—than from your parents themselves.

To conduct business on your parents' behalf, you'll need to see a lawyer and draw up a durable power of attorney. But you'll need to consult with siblings first, as this will avoid conflict later. If they protest, you might want to seek family counseling or hire a professional financial advisor to help with big financial decisions. Either way, consulting a financial advisor can help you find ways to make the most of what money your parents have.

⟡ Respect Your Parents' Need to Control Some Money

When you talk to your parents about finances, be comforting. Tell them that you have hired a professional who can help you pay off the bills, stop creditors from calling, and see that they'll have as much money as possible to pay for their care. Just as important, let them know that you won't control *all* of the money—just what is needed for major purchases and essential living expenses, both now and in the future. Assure them that they will still have some money to do with as they wish.

Because managing one's own money is equated with independence and security in our society, having control over at least some of their money is important to your parents. If they still get out, allow them some spending money or speak to your credit card company about getting them a companion card on your account with a low limit. That way, your parents can make small purchases without the danger or losing cash or charging big-ticket items they neither want nor need. With a companion card to your account, the bill comes directly to you, so that you can pay it yourself and monitor purchases, if necessary.

I Know My Mom Is Manipulating Me, but How Can I Stop It?

When you were a child, your parents may have gained your cooperation with threats of sending you to bed without dinner, shipping you off to boarding school, or the infamous, "Just wait till your father gets home."

Just because you've grown up doesn't mean that the threats end. When controlling parents can no longer control their children with the prospect of spankings or lost privileges, they look for other ways to exert control even to the extreme of threatening their own demise. In essence, they say, "If you dare do anything enjoyable that doesn't involve me, *then you obviously don't care whether I live or die.*"

You know that's not the truth; even manipulative parents know it's not true, yet the tactic works wonders with some daughters. Some women have sacrificed jobs, family time, rest, and recreation fearing disapproval from their parents or the guilt they would experience if, by chance, their parent *did* happen to die while they were doing something for themselves.

Susan, who was one of three girls in her family, was determined not to be one of those women. Ever since she was a young child, Susan had always been eager to please her critical parents. Her parents knew it and took advantage of her good nature. When her sisters argued over who would get the window seats in the car, Susan's parents always placed her in the middle; they knew she wouldn't complain. If there was enough money in the family budget for one prom dress or one kid to go to camp, Susan never demanded it, and one of her sisters always got it. When her parents doled out the household chores, Susan always seemed to get more than her share, and she did them promptly without argument.

When Susan turned fifty-five and her mother began having health problems, nothing much had changed. Susan took on the responsibility of caring for her mother with little complaint. She did everything she could to meet her mother's demands, putting her own life and family on hold—until her husband, eager to get his wife back, purchased tickets for the two of them to spend their twenty-fifth wedding anniversary on a cruise.

Knowing that being away for seven days would upset her mother, she started preparing the month before. "I arranged for friends to check on her each day and for a cleaning service to come by and clean her apartment one day while I was gone. I promised to prepare some meals ahead, and I lined up friends and family members who agreed to be on call, if my mother needed them."

Rather than being pleased that her daughter had made great efforts to be sure she was cared for, the woman sulked. "She told me, 'You know I'm not well. If I die while you're gone, at least I will die knowing that *you* are having fun,' " Susan said.

Susan really didn't think her mother would die while she was gone. If she believed that, she wouldn't have agreed to the trip. She thought several times about canceling but, despite daily threats from her mother Susan decided to stand firm. "I have appeased her all my life," she said. "Now I want to spend time with my husband."

Susan took her trip as planned and—not surprisingly—her mother was alive when she returned. In fact, over the next several years, Susan took many more trips despite her mother's threats. Ten years after the cruise her mother is still alive and still complaining.

Situations like Susan's are unfortunate but common. Whether your parent's threats are as overt as Susan's mother's or more subtle, realize one thing: No one can manipulate you unless you allow them to. Sure, your parent is trying to manipulate you, but whether his or her tactics work is entirely up to you. By constantly playing into your parent's hands, you are enabling the manipulative behavior.

To stop the cycle, gently but firmly tell your parent you cannot meet such unrealistic demands and that you will not allow him or her to threaten you. If you are your parent's primary caregiver, certainly you should arrange for someone else to provide that care when you are not available, but beyond that, try to enjoy time away from your parent on occasion. Taking even a short break to pursue your own interests or other relationships will make you a more effective caregiver when you return.

How Can I Bring up the Topic of My Parent's Will?

One of the most sensitive subjects you may ever have to discuss with your parent is his or her wishes for dividing property after death. The mere mention of a will implies that death is coming (as it is for all of us, eventually, but not too many of us want to talk about it). And talking about death and money in the same breath can seem mercenary.

Ideally, the time to discuss potentially explosive or upsetting topics is when your parent is healthy and independent. Bringing up the subject of a will, for example, seems less threatening when your parent's death isn't imminent, and discussing your parent's future living arrangements is less stressful when you don't need to decide something immediately. Any decision is easier when all of the involved parties are somewhat relaxed and healthy.

If your parent has a considerable amount of property and you seem concerned about a will, he or she may worry that you just want to get your share. If your parent has never had much or has exhausted his or her finances paying for long-term care, he or she may feel bad that there is nothing to leave the family. This is a sensitive subject, to say the least.

When you are forced to finally talk about a will, acknowledge how difficult the conversation is for *you*. You might say, "Mom, this isn't something I want to talk about or even think about, but I think it's important that we discuss it. I think you need to draw up a will. It's not that I am concerned about your money—I hope you know I would rather have you with me than have all the money in the world. But I do want to make sure that your money and possessions are someday distributed the way you want them to be."

Let your mother know that without a will, the laws of the state set forth how her estate will be divided. Also let her know that without a will her heirs will likely end up paying more state tax and, in some cases, more federal tax on their inheritance.

If you think your parent might have trouble getting to a lawyer's office to draw up a legal will, that shouldn't be an issue. Many law firms and organizations will send someone to your parent's home to gather the information and then return the completed will for your parent's signature. Check with your local legal aid society to find a firm or organization that provides this service, and ask your parent if he or she would be more comfortable if you sat in on the meeting. You can help answer—and ask—questions, provide moral support for your parent, and be mindful of anything that doesn't seem right. Unfortunately, many less-than-reputable businesses prey on vulnerable seniors.

If your parent is relatively well and still able to make rational decisions, now is the time to bring up a will. Be proactive. Don't wait until he or she is on heavy pain medication, unable to think clearly, or near death. Trying to draw up a will during those circumstances will be extremely difficult for you both. Furthermore, the courts may not accept a will prepared under those circumstances and may divide the property as if there were no will.

How Can I Even Begin to Discuss My Parent's End-of-Life Wishes?

She wants to donate her body to science; you want her in a plot next to your father where you can take flowers on Mother's Day. You want to take her to a medical center halfway across the country where doctors may be able to treat her cancer and keep her alive a few months longer; she wants to let the disease run its course and die quietly in her own home.

If you've ever gotten into these discussions about end-of-life wishes, you're already way ahead of many caregivers and their elderly parents. The thought of losing a parent is so painful that most caregivers hesitate to even bring up the subject of death. But if you want to abide by your parent's last wishes, it's important that you initiate the conversation if they don't. The best time to do discuss end-of-life issues is before the end is imminent and when your parent is still able to make rational decisions. If your parent is dying or has been diagnosed with a terminal disease, the discussion becomes more urgent and is likely to be much more stressful. Even worse, if your parent becomes unable to speak, and you have not discussed these issues beforehand, you're left with difficult decisions—and possibly disagreements with siblings—regarding not knowing what he or she would have wanted.

To ensure that your parents' wishes are respected, ask them to draw up a living will and a medical power of attorney (also called a durable power of attorney for health care or health care directive). The living will is a document that states their wishes for end-of-life care, including life support and organ donation. The medical power of attorney authorizes a trusted friend or family member to carry out wishes stated in the living will. The purpose of a living will is to allow a person to make a decision regarding the final days and hours of life if he or she is unable to speak. Also, if your parent wishes not to be resuscitated (given CPR) if his or her heart and lungs stop, complete a Do Not Resuscitate (DNR) request and keep it handy. Having a copy of your parent's DNR request in an accessible place will ensure that your parent's wishes are honored, even if you can't quickly get to the other legal documents.

When initiating the discussion with your parent, start slowly. Jim Towley, president of Aging with Dignity, a nonprofit organization that provides families with advice and legal tools to ensure wishes of older people and their loved ones are respected, recommends avoiding tough subjects—like DNR orders, feeding tubes, and ventilators—at least in the beginning. Rather, he suggests you start by asking your parents about music, poetry, and long-loved sounds that would be peaceful and comforting to them at the end. After you talk about easy subjects, you can work into some of the more difficult ones.

For most family caregivers, knowing the family member has already made those decisions is a relief. It helps you avoid guessing or having to make those difficult decisions later when emotions are at an all-time high.

On the other hand, if you think you may have difficulty carrying out your parent's wishes, let him or her know. Someone less involved emotionally may be a better choice to hold this position of seeing that the living will is carried out. Even if you disagree with your parent about the final days of life and the immediate time thereafter, if he or she is capable of making those decisions, do your best to abide by them.

In most cases, abiding by a parent's wishes is much less difficult than bringing up the subject to start with. If your family member feels uncomfortable about drawing up a legal document to state his or her wishes, you might suggest that you can have a living will prepared for yourself simultaneously. This will not only make your parent feel more comfortable, but it will also be helpful to your own children or caregivers when the time comes.

I Think My Mother Is Severely Depressed—What Should I Do?

Depression is common among older people. Although 6 to 10 percent of older adults meet the criteria for a diagnosis of clinical depression, psychologists estimate that at least a third of all people over age sixty-five have depressive symptoms that are severe enough to interfere with their daily lives. These symptoms can have many causes—from the loss of a spouse or other loved one to living day to day with a chronic health condition. In fact, some problems—including some strokes and Parkinson's disease—have been found to directly affect the mood centers of the brain.

Regardless of the cause of depression, the result is often the same. It robs people of the joy of life in later years and can lead to other health problems. In the worst of cases, depression leads to suicide. People over sixty-five have a suicide rate that is six times that of younger people. The greatest risk, experts say, is among white men over eighty-five.

Clearly, treatment for depression is necessary. And in most cases, it is highly effective—if the older person gets treatment. But that's a big *if*. Unfortunately, many older people are reluctant to seek help. Some flat-out refuse it.

After Linda's father died, her mother never seemed quite the same. For a while, Linda attributed her mother's uncharacteristic behavior to the normal grieving process. After all, her parents had been married for almost fifty-three years. But after a year had passed and her mother still refused to eat much, go out with her friends, or even get out of bed some days, Linda knew something more was wrong. Linda's mother was depressed.

"When I told my mother I was worried about her—that maybe she needed to speak with someone or get some medication to help her feel better, she acted like I had insulted her," Linda recalls. "She said she wasn't crazy—she was just sad, and that one day when [my husband] Chuck died, I'd know how she felt."

If you have an older parent who may need psychiatric care yet has refused it, or you've been afraid to suggest it, it may help to get a third party involved.

Linda started by having a talk with her mother's primary doctor. She told him how her mother's behavior had changed, and he agreed that it sounded like depression. He also agreed to bring up the subject at her mother's next appointment and to direct her toward the help that he felt would be most appropriate after talking with her.

As it turned out, the primary doctor was able to prescribe antidepressant medication that helped Linda's mother. By telling her that many of his patients were on the medication—particularly the older women who just didn't have much energy anymore—she agreed to try it. She also agreed to speak with her clergy, which was less intimidating to her than seeing a "mental health professional."

The same technique may be useful for older people who need the specialized help of a geriatric psychiatrist. If you can have your parent's primary doctor broach the subject and make the appointment with the doctor, he or she may be more agreeable than if you are the one to make the recommendation.

If going through your parent's doctor doesn't help, make an appointment with a mental health professional yourself and bring your loved one along. Tell your parent that the stresses in life are affecting you too and that it might be helpful for both of you to see someone together. After a visit or two with you, your parent may be willing to go it alone. If not, you may wish to continue together—particularly if unresolved issues between the two of you are contributing to the depression.

If all else fails, there may be alternatives to having your parent meet with a psychiatrist face-to-face. Your parent's doctor may be able to arrange for a psychiatrist to view and assess a videotape of your parent. You make the videotape, deliver it to the doctor, and he or she uses it to help make an assessment. Another option is telemedicine. Some highly specialized medical centers offer this service for residents of senior centers and people in rural areas who are unable to get to the psychiatrist. Using a personal computer and real-time audio and video connections, your loved one can see and speak with the psychiatrist—and the psychiatrist can see and speak with him or her—without an actual office visit.

While Linda's mother was helped a lot by the antidepressant her doctor prescribed, antidepressants aren't for everyone. Often seniors can benefit from counseling or "talk therapy" designed to uncover the reasons of their depression and find ways to address and deal with those issues. If your parent is up to it, you might want to look into group therapy (essentially a support group facilitated by a psychologist, counselor, social worker, or other professional, which may be less intimidating and less expensive than individual therapy). If your parent can't attend group meetings, see if he or she might attend one with you online.

If your parent's doctor does prescribe an antidepressant, don't be alarmed or allow your siblings to make your parent feel that taking medication is unnecessary or somehow shameful. There's a large variety of antidepressants today that are widely prescribed and safer for older people than earlier versions. What's most important is that your parent gets the help he or she needs to function optimally and enjoy life again.

One word of caution: Many drugs can interact negatively with other drugs. Antidepressants, for example, may increase the effects of other drugs that depress the central nervous system, such as antihistamines and narcotic pain medications. For elderly people, who are often on many different drugs, the potential for drug interactions is great. Be sure to let your parent's doctor know all of the medications he or she is already taking before another drug is added to the mix.

How Can I Deal with My Increasingly Forgetful Parent?

One day, on the way home from a quick trip to the supermarket, Annette's father asked why she had made a right turn instead of a left turn. "You have to make a left to get to Tremont, Annie," he told her. Tremont was the street where her family had lived for forty-seven years, the street where Annette herself had grown up. But her father hadn't lived on Tremont Street for the past five years—ever since he moved across town to live with his fifty-one-year-old daughter and her husband.

"I gently told my father that he didn't live on Tremont anymore, that he lived on Creekside Court with me and Jack," Annette said. "But it didn't sink in. Over the following months, he told me time and again that he lived on Tremont. When I reminded him otherwise, he became agitated and angry."

For the caregiver of a person with memory loss, a loved one's insistence that things are exactly the way they were five years ago—or perhaps never were—can be enough to make you feel like *you're* going crazy. While you may think it's important to bring them back to the present (or to reality) to preserve what memory they have left, doing so might not help. And, as Annette found, it can lead to conflict. Although this is not advis-

able in all situations, sometimes you can avoid a lot of unnecessary anger if you just go along. Let them live in their own world.
At the same time, if they're making constant requests (such as
asking you to take them home to a place they no longer live or
to walk a dog or call a friend who died years ago), creatively
look for ways to divert their attention, put them off, or make it
seem as if you have already done what they ask.

Once Annette decided to go along with her father, she found
his insistence to go back to Tremont Street lessened. "The next
time my father insisted I take him to Tremont, I told him I
would take him there soon, but first I would like to bring him
to my house for lunch because I had lots of leftovers in the refrigerator and my husband, Jack, was looking forward to seeing
him."

Instead of being agitated, Annette's father seemed happy to
be going on another outing, and by the time they had finished
lunch, he had forgotten all about Tremont.

What Can I Do about My Parent's Bad Behavior?

Open your home to an aging loved one and you just may be
opening Pandora's box.

Shelly learned that lesson the hard way when she and her
husband invited her eighty-year-old mother-in-law to move in
with her family. Living in separate states, they didn't see each
other too often and when they did, their visits were usually
pleasant but brief. So she wasn't prepared for what was to
come.

"We had a wonderful relationship until she arrived," Shelly
said. "But as soon as she got here, my business became her business, and nothing I did was right. My house was not clean

enough, my meals were not nutritious enough, and I didn't plan my time well enough."

If Shelly went to the gym in the evening, her mother-in-law criticized her for being self-centered. If she failed to answer questions with "yes, ma'am," her mother-in-law told her she was disrespectful. If she allowed her children to stay up past their bedtimes, her mother-in-law accused her of being permissive. If she took her husband's shirts to the laundry instead of washing and pressing them herself, she was being lazy.

After two months of her mother-in-law's rudeness, Shelly said she was ready to ship her mother-in-law (and her husband, who did little to help the situation) off to a retirement home—maybe in Siberia!

Though Shelly's case may seem a bit extreme, it's not unusual. Older parents who move in with grown children often feel they deserve to call the shots. Even though you are grown and perfectly capable of managing your own life, they still see you (or your husband) as their child.

Parents who were critical when they were younger may be even more critical now—remember that personality traits are magnified as you age! Parents who tried to respect your opinions or hold back their criticism when you were growing up may be less inhibited about speaking up, especially if they have some type of cognitive impairment.

Before you tell your critical mother-in-law where to go (Siberia or elsewhere), for example, consider what she's going through. Regardless of whether she gave up her own home to live with you or she's just seeing you more because she's more dependent on you, remember that she has lost much of the control over her own life. Her only grasp of control may be in trying to control your life or control you. If you cave in to her criticisms or lose your temper, she may feel she has succeeded. On the other hand, her criticism may be well intended. After all, she did things differently from you and had a well-run home, a happy husband, and perfect children (in her eyes, anyway!). She wants the same for you. Or perhaps not. Maybe she regrets mistakes she made with her own family and somehow thinks she is sparing you from doing the same. Or perhaps she harbors anger at you for taking away her son or because of a family conflict from years earlier.

If you are able to have a heart-to-heart talk with the family member who is criticizing you, you may discover some reasons behind her behavior—or you may not. At least you can take the time to let her know how you feel, but do so calmly. Let her know gently but firmly that while you appreciate her advice (even if you don't), this is your home and you prefer to do things your own way. She had her chance to raise her kids, keep her house, and do her husband's laundry. Now it's your turn to do the same.

If your parent shows improvement—any improvement—in her criticism, respond positively. Even if you just agree on which laundry detergent to use, that's a start. Sometimes agreeing on small things will give her an increased sense of control that will lead to greater cooperation on the bigger things.

You may find it helps to give your parent a little slack—or at least some control in small family decisions. If she wants chicken for dinner one night, why not prepare it or, if she's able, let her do it. If you go out to dinner, let her pick the restaurant. If she doesn't like the television programs you watch, let her choose the program some nights, or get her her own TV to watch in her room. If she doesn't approve of your housekeeping and she's able, let her help with dusting and mopping. Sometimes little changes can make a big difference.

If the criticism continues or interferes with the well-being of your family, however, only you and your family can decide whether to ignore it or insist she stop—or move elsewhere.

How Can I Avoid Feeling Jealous of My Sibling?

You're there every day, caring for your father, taking him to his doctor's appointments, shopping for his groceries, picking up his prescriptions, and scheduling his therapy. But when your younger sister—who lives three states away and sees him maybe once a year—comes for a visit, she's the most wonderful daughter on earth. And, well, you're left feeling completely taken for granted.

It's common for one woman to provide the vast majority of care for her parent but for another child in the family—even one who does virtually nothing to help his or her parent—to be the apple of the parent's eye. Like a cat that walks past its eager owner to climb into the lap of someone who wants nothing to do with it, parents sometimes gravitate toward siblings who appear to care the least.

When this happens, women who provide a parent's daily care may feel like the dutiful son in the parable of the prodigal son. In the familiar story, the son who ran away and squandered his inheritance on wine and women was welcomed home by his father with gold jewelry and a fattened calf, while the son who had faithfully stayed by his father's side all along couldn't even get a goat to share with his friends.

As the dutiful daughter, you may wish you could tell your parent the truth about your sister—that she's involved with a married man, that she smoked pot in college, and that she was the one who put the dent in your dad's '67 Chevy.

As much as you might like to say things to make your siblings look bad, don't. Pointing your sister or brother out to be the jerk that you think they are (and may well be) is only hurtful to your parent—and puts you on par with a mudslinger in a political race. Whatever bad you have to say will only hurt your paernt's opinion of *you*. Chances are, your parent already knows the truth about your sibling and knows he or she would be in pretty bad shape if he or she ever had to depend on that child.

If you must say something to your parent to point out your constant caregiving role, put a positive spin on it. For example, you might say, "I know how much you enjoy it when Suzy comes to visit, but I'm glad I get to be with you every day."

Also, before you get too angry with your parent about the preferential treatment toward your sibling, think about your own behavior in a similar situation. Aren't you more solicitous toward old friends, acquaintances, and even strangers than to those who mean the most in your day-to-day life? If your spouse or best friend calls you on the phone when you're in the middle of something important, for example, you probably wouldn't hesitate to say, "Can I call you back?" before you really know why they're calling. If an old friend you haven't heard from since college called, would you do the same?

Good or bad, we are often more polite and accommodating to people we rarely or never see than we are to the people who are closest to us.

As for your errant sibling, if caregiving without that help becomes too much for you, don't expect those once-a-year visits to become weekly. But do offer the opportunity to do more to help out, and have some specific suggestions in mind. To your sibling, *you* may seem like the perfect daughter who needs no help. He or she may be just as jealous (yes, jealous!) of you. If your sibling can't or won't participate with the hands-on care, at least suggest he or she help you pay for some respite care.

How Can I Convince My Parent to Slow Down?

When Lucy's mother's congestive heart failure became so severe that she became winded just walking from the kitchen to the bedroom in her small apartment, Lucy insisted that her mother move in with her and her family. "Essentially Mom's doctor told us that her heart had a limited number of beats left," Lucy recalls. "The more she exerted herself, the sooner she would use up those beats." By having her mother close and taking care of her, Lucy reasoned, she would conserve her mother's heart as much as possible. So she was horrified when her mother insisted on helping her load the washing machine, mop the kitchen floor, or sweep the back porch.

For many older people, sitting still when there's work to be done isn't easy. Relaxing while another person—particularly their child—does that work is even harder. So how do you keep an eager older parent from overdoing it?

Lucy solved the problem by finding some sedentary chores for her mother to do, such as folding laundry on the sofa, chopping or mixing food at the kitchen table, and clipping coupons from the Sunday paper. "All of these not only helped me, but they filled her time and gave her a sense of participating in the family."

Lucy also encouraged her mother to spend time with Lucy's two children. "I told her the time she spent playing card games or watching videos with her grandchildren was far more important than any housework," she said.

When an older loved one insists on doing more than he or she physically should, gently let your parent know that you value him or her more than any chores done to help you. At the same time, find chores that aren't physically strenuous that he or she can do easily. That way, you get some much-needed help and your parent gets the sense of usefulness he or she craves. (For more information on techniques and products that can make daily activities more doable, see Chapter 5.)

❧ *Eleven tips to avoid head-butting* ❧

You can't eliminate all disagreements and uncomfortable situations with your parents, but you can often resolve conflicts and make your relationship run more smoothly, if you just know how. The following eleven tips can help.

1. *Start early.* There are some issues that almost all caregivers or would-be caregivers will face at some point, including changing living arrangements (e.g. moving your parent to an assisted-living center or a relative's home), drawing up a will, or giving up driving. If they haven't arisen, discussing them with your family member before decisions must be made can be less stressful. Furthermore, if you are considering a nursing home or assisted-living center, you may need to get on a waiting list a year or two before you're ready to make the move—particularly if your parent is on Medicaid. Most centers that accept Medicaid patients accept only a few, so the waiting lists for those limited spots are longer.

2. *Pick your battles.* As a caregiver, you will likely encounter situations where you have to override your parent's wishes to keep them safe and well. But do so only when necessary. If your father wants to drive his car after his license has been revoked, for example, it's your responsibility to stop him. If he wants to wear red plaid pants with a blue striped shirt or put up his Christmas tree in August, let it slide.

3. *Enlist the help of professionals.* Even though you may be closer to your parent than anyone else, that doesn't mean you have to be the bearer of all bad news. If you think your parent needs to see a psychiatrist or trade her high-heel pumps for safer shoes, for example, have a trusted doctor broach the subject.

4. *Let your parents live in his or her own world.* If your father's college football stories or your mother's insistence that she's never met your husband (despite the fact she's known him for thirty years!) drives you up a wall, don't let on. How many times has your child or best friend told you the same story over and over? Try acting amazed when you hear about that winning touchdown for the thousandth time or tell your mother that you'd love to introduce her to your husband (just make sure you let him in on the role playing!).

5. *Don't make assumptions.* If you need to make a decision regarding your loved one's care, don't assume you know what's best for him or her. For example, one article I read recently said that most caregivers thought their parent would be better off moving in with them, while most older people said they would prefer to stay in their own homes or live in an assisted-living center. In other words, Dad may prefer living in familiar surroundings or with friends his own age to living with you in your home. If your parent is mentally able to participate in decisions regarding care, ask for his or her input.

6. *Consider your parent's feelings.* It's not easy getting old. When you think of things from your parent's perspective—and consider that you may well be in that situation one day—it's easier to smooth over bad feelings that might lead to conflict and simply forgive.

7. *Allow your parent to call the shots—sometimes.* Many of the conflicts that arise in caregiving come when parents feel they are no longer useful or in control. As with parenting your own child, it's important to give your parents some control in the family—particularly if he or she lives in your home with your family. If possible, allow him or her to plan meals, or pick TV shows or family activities now and then. Also, as much as your parent is able, encourage him or her to do tasks that help the family—such as helping to keep house, fold laundry, or pack school lunches.

8. *Use positive reinforcement.* It's easy to complain when things aren't going right, especially when you are overwhelmed and exhausted. But instead of complaining when things go wrong, try praising your parent when things go right. Chances are your parent wants to please you and will appreciate the encouragement.

9. *Foster your parent's independence.* Some older people sit back and wish to be waited on. But many would much rather do things themselves—if they can. By helping your parent do the things he or she can, you can help boost self-esteem. An added benefit for you: You'll free up some time for yourself and escape the criticism that can come when you don't do things exactly to your parent's liking.

10. *Take time for yourself.* Even minor conflicts can escalate to epic proportions when you're faced with them day in and day out. One key to being an effective caregiver, and minimizing head-butting, is to take a break now and then. Go out with friends, take a long walk, find activities that you enjoy *without* your parent. When you get back, you'll be in a better frame of mind to deal with whatever comes your way.

11. *Reconsider your arrangements.* If constant conflicts with your parent are having a negative impact on your health and your family, you may have no choice but to make other arrangements for your parent's care. If he or she is living in your house, perhaps your parent could move in with another family member or into an assisted-living home. If you are providing most of the care outside your home, perhaps another family member could take over some of the duties. Whether you remain the primary caretaker or not, it's important that you still stay involved in your parent's life.

As you try to navigate the emotional minefields of caregiving, be aware that some head-butting is inevitable. The shift in roles—from the person providing care for the child to a person needing help from the child—is understandably frustrating for older adults. Be patient. Minimize frustrations as much as possible by keeping your aging loved ones involved in the decisions that affect their lives. Always allow and encourage them to do what they can for themselves.

In Chapter 5, we'll look at the importance of helping your parents maintain their independence—for their own sake and yours—as well as some simple steps and devices that will help them do more for themselves and relieve some of the burden from you.

Five

HOW CAN I FOSTER MY PARENT'S INDEPENDENCE?

Many women tell me they feel bad that they aren't doing enough for their aging mom or dad. But surprisingly, what I find quite often is that women do *too much* for their parents. That is, they spend time and energy doing tasks that, with a little help and encouragement, their parents could do for themselves. While these women think they are helping their parents (and many parents fall into a comfortable pattern of being helped), they are actually depriving their parents of independence—and overtaxing themselves. Being a caregiver doesn't always mean taking care of your parent's every need 24/7. It sometimes means *more* to provide your parent with the tools to live independently and then letting him or her do the rest.

Whether you have already fallen into the pattern of doing too much or you want to avoid this trend in the future, it may take delicacy, tact, creativity, and, in some cases, cool gadgets and devices to help your parent become more independent.

I have found that most older people encounter at least one—and often several—of six main barriers to independence: vision problems, hearing problems, balance and mobility problems, gripping and dexterity problems, cognition and memory loss, and emotional problems. Let's take a look at a further explanation of each of these barriers and delve into the products and methods that will help parents experiencing these challenges become more self-sufficient—a win-win situation.

Vision Problems

As we age, virtually all of us will experience changes in our vision. The most common change is *presbyopia*, the inability to see things clearly up close. By the time we are in our forties, most of us begin to notice presbyopia. (In fact, if you are holding this book at arm's length to read it—and wishing your arms were longer—you are probably already familiar with this all too common problem!) Presbyopia occurs when age-related changes to the eye's lens cause it to harden and become less flexible. Usually the right pair of reading glasses can help compensate for this problem.

Major Causes of Vision Loss

In addition to presbyopia, which virtually all of us experience to some degree, there are four major causes of vision loss in older adults:

MACULAR DEGENERATION
The leading cause of blindness in the Western world, age-related macular degeneration occurs when there is damage to the cen-

tral part of the retina (the back layer of the inside of the eye that records the images we see and sends them via the optic nerve to be registered in the brain). This part of the retina, called the macula, is responsible for central vision and controls our ability to focus and recognize color and detail. People with macular degeneration may be unable to drive, read, or even recognize faces. Age-related macular degeneration affects approximately one in 500 of people between the ages of fifty-five and sixty-four, and rises to 13 percent of people over age eighty-five. There are two types of macular degeneration: dry and wet. Dry macular degeneration, the most common form, comes on slowly and often subtly. Wet macular degeneration comes on suddenly when blood vessels leak in or under the retina. It generally begins as a large black dot in the center of vision and progresses quickly.

Unfortunately, once macular degeneration begins, it cannot be reversed. However, your parent (and you) may be able to minimize their risk of macular degeneration by managing diabetes, cholesterol levels, and blood pressure and by avoiding cigarettes and excessive exposure to UV light.

Recent research suggests that older people who suffer from macular degeneration may be able to train their eyes to take advantage of their peripheral vision by looking slightly away from the object of interest so that they are using undamaged parts of the retina to see.

In a small study at the University of Illinois at Chicago College of Medicine, researchers administered a test in which letters and numbers flashed randomly in the periphery of participants' vision. Using the data they gathered, the researchers created a profile of each patient's visual acuity at twenty-seven locations within the retina and then devised an eight-week course of eye exercises to help each participant use the parts of their retinas that worked best.

The results were promising: Most of the participants improved their vision significantly and increased their ability to "navigate in the real world," reports Janet P. Szylk, the psychophysicist who led the study. Though the study was confined to just a small group of people, it offers hope for others with macular degeneration who are concerned that vision loss will severely limit their ability to navigate their surroundings and enjoy life.

GLAUCOMA

Glaucoma is damage to the optic nerve, usually caused by the buildup of fluid pressure within the eye. Results of the damage may be subtle at first. As it progresses, however, glaucoma can cause loss of peripheral vision.

Fortunately, glaucoma can be detected through two routine tests: tonometry and ophthalmoscopy. The tonometry test involves giving drops to numb the eye and then using a device to measure the eye's inner pressure. Ophthalmoscopy uses a special instrument to illuminate and magnify the inside of the eye so the doctor can examine the optic nerve. If one of those tests detects glaucoma, the doctor may use other tests to confirm the diagnosis and determine the extent of the problem.

Approximately 2.2 million Americans have been diagnosed with glaucoma, and an estimated 2 million more have it who don't know it. The Glaucoma Research Foundation recommends glaucoma screenings at age thirty-five and forty, every two to four years after age forty, and every one to two years after age sixty.

Although the actual vision loss is irreversible, detecting and treating the problem early may keep it from progressing. A number of prescription medications are available to treat glaucoma.

CATARACTS

A cataract is a clouding of the eye's lens—the part that focuses light and is responsible producing clear images—that can cause hazy vision and make the eyes more sensitive to glare. As the cataract progresses, your parent may find it difficult to read or to distinguish between similar colors.

Although macular degeneration is the leading cause of blindness in older people in the Western world, cataracts are the leading cause of blindness worldwide. In the United States, cataracts are a common cause of vision impairment, affecting nearly 20.5 million people age forty and older. By age eighty, more than half of all Americans develop cataracts.

Aside from advanced age, risk factors for cataracts include diabetes, alcoholism, and certain medications including corticosteroid medications such as prednisone. Treatment for cataracts involves removing the damaged lens and replacing it with a clear synthetic one. This surgery is performed routinely, and with great success.

DIABETIC RETINOPATHY

Diabetic retinopathy is a complication of advanced diabetes caused by the leaking of blood vessels into the retina. Symptoms can include blurred vision and the inability to see things up close.

Nearly half of all people with diabetes will eventually develop some degree of diabetic retinopathy. The risk increases over time. Diabetic retinopathy can be largely prevented through careful monitoring and control of blood sugar levels. Once diabetic retinopathy has begun, laser treatment of local areas to stop the bleeding may help keep it from progressing.

Regardless of the problem that causes it, impaired vision can take a serious toll on an older person's quality of life. It can affect the ability to read, enjoy leisure activities such as needlework and TV, or even get around the house safely. But that doesn't mean your parent can't do these things at all—or certainly that you have to do everything for him or her.

In many cases, appropriate medical treatment—or a good pair of corrective lenses—can help improve your parent's vision. There is also a wide array of products that can restore independence to people with impaired vision. Let's take a look at some simple things you can do to help your parent cope with vision problems and a sampling of the many products available for them.

Five Tips to Cope with Aging Eyes

1. **See the eye doctor regularly.** For both vision and eye health, it's important for your parent to see the eye doctor regularly. Regular checkups ensure that the eyeglass prescription is kept up to date and that any potentially vision-robbing condition can be identified and, if possible, treated before it causes irreparable damage.

2. **Maintain glasses.** An older man I knew was complaining that his vision was going fast. Even *with* his glasses, he could not see as well as he did just a few months before. Everything was blurry. When his daughter examined his glasses, the reason for his blurry vision was clear: His glasses *weren't*. Apparently, he had tried to clean them with a kitchen cleaner that had left them smeary. Once she cleaned them with clear water and a soft cloth,

his vision improved instantly. Needless to say, it's important to make sure your parent's glasses are clean and in good repair.

3. **Buy big.** From large-print books to oversized playing cards and TV screens, big items are a big help to older people with low vision. Bigger is easier to see, and larger versions of items they already use may make it easier for your parent to continue activities they enjoy. If you can't get something bigger, make it *look* bigger. All sorts of magnifying devices may make that possible. (For a list of both bigger products and magnifying devices, see pages 231–237.)

4. **Keep it light.** As anyone past forty can attest, a bright light becomes necessary for reading or doing fine work such as coin or stamp collecting or jewelry making. For a parent with low vision, good lighting only makes hobbies easier, it is also essential for preventing falls and accidents. If your parent will be traveling and staying in a hotel or with friends or relatives, have him or her take along night-lights to light unfamiliar surroundings or a few high-wattage lightbulbs to replace dimmer bulbs at their destination. One word of caution: Before replacing bulbs in any small lamp, check for a warning (often printed inside the shade) against using bulbs of over forty or sixty watts. Using a high wattage bulb where it doesn't belong could potentially start a fire.

5. **Organize and rearrange.** If you find it hard to locate things in a messy house or almost trip over stacks of magazines or shoes left on the floor, imagine how hard it would be to maneuver such obstacles if you couldn't see well. Helping your parent clean up and put things in their proper places will not only make needed items easier to find, it will also make the house safer.

Products for the Visually Impaired

Products for the visually impaired generally fall into one of three categories: those that are oversized, those that magnify, and those that talk (or listen). Here are some of my favorites.

OVERSIZED PRODUCTS

A variety of oversized products are available to help seniors with low vision live more independently. Some good sources for oversized products:

www.goldviolin.com
www.independentliving.com
www.largeprintbooks.com
www.cordless-phones-america.com
www.twacomm.com
and www.eldercorner.com

• **Large-print publications.** Many books, magazines, and even newspapers, including the *New York Times*, come in large-print versions that are easier on aging eyes. Some Web sites for seniors and people with vision impairments feature large print as well.

• **Playing cards.** Thanks to oversized playing cards, there's no need for your parent to forgo a game of bridge or solitaire, even if he or she has a hard time seeing standard-sized playing cards. Oversized cards feature large numbers and symbols and are color-coded. Even if your parent has trouble seeing the large numbers, he or she can quickly memorize the colors associated with each suit and number.

• **Telephones.** Many older adults don't pick up the phone to maintain important social ties because they can't see to dial the numbers. Phones with oversized keypads are easier for aging eyes to see. An added bonus: They're easier for less-than-nimble hands to press. At least one model I have found even "says" the numbers back as your loved one presses them, virtually eliminating dialing wrong numbers.

• **Television remotes.** No more fumbling with the TV controls or squinting to see those tiny numbers on the traditional remote control. Some large remotes have easy-to-see light-up buttons. Not only for seniors, these larger models are great for any of us who occasionally lose a remote in the sofa cushions. (Kids love them too!)

MAGNIFYING PRODUCTS

If you can't get a bigger version of something your parent needs or enjoys, make the existing product look bigger with a magnifying device. The most obvious choice, of course, is the traditional handheld magnifying glass. But if your parent has severe vision loss or if low vision interferes with his or her ability to do favorite activities, there are many specialized devices that can help. Check out electronic and medical equipment stores as well as the following websites:

www.freedomofspeech.com
www.brent-krueger.com
www.delpozzo.com
www.sharperimage.com
www.productsforseniors.com

Here are a few of my favorites:

• **Television magnifier.** This device fits directly over the TV screen. The smallest I have seen can magnify a thirteen- or fourteen-inch screen to twenty-two inches, but these devices come in a variety of sizes to fit your parent's TV. A similar device is available to magnify computer monitors.

• **Magnifying lamps.** These handy lamps, placed on a desk or bedside table, not only enlarge what you need to see, they illuminate it. They can be helpful for looking up phone numbers, reading, or seeing to thread a needle. What a great idea!

• **Crafter's magnifier.** Suspended from a cord or plastic piece around the neck, this oversized magnifying glass rests perpendicularly against your chest to offer hands-free magnification for reading or handiwork.

• **Closed-Circuit Television (CCTV) system.** To make small print and images really large, plug this handheld scanner into the back of your parent's TV. He or she can scan in small print and pictures from books, brochures, and newspapers and see them on the TV screen—at up to twenty-eight times the original size!

TALKING PRODUCTS

If your parent has difficulty seeing but his or her hearing is still pretty good, why not try a product that talks, eliminating the need to make out small numbers and letters on clocks, books, and even appliance controls? Here are some items you might want to check out. You can find these and others at some medical supply stores and through the following Web sites:

www.independentliving.com
www.main99.com
www.assistedaccess.com
www.lowvision.org
www.nanopac.com
www.harriscomm.com
www.viguide.com

• **Watches and clocks.** Does your parent have to squint to see the numbers on the bedside clock? Is it impossible for your parent to read a wristwatch? A wide selection of timepieces can audibly tell the time at the press of a button. Some automatically announce the time on the hour. Another clock I've seen projects the time in large numbers on the wall or ceiling.

• **Audio books.** If your parent loves a good book but can't read the fine print, a wide selection of books are available on cassette tape. You may purchase his or her favorites online or at many bookstores. But first, you might want to check with your local library, where you can check them out for free!

• **Kitchen appliances.** Is the keypad on the microwave too hard to read? Treat your mother to a microwave that tells her the time and cook level she is pressing and then informs her when her food is ready. Other gadgets she may find helpful in the kitchen include a talking measuring cup, kitchen scale, and timer.

• **Money identifier.** If your parent insists on carrying cash but has a hard time identifying bills when a purchase is made, a money identifier can audibly tell the denomination of any bill being used. At a price point of four hundred dollars, however, this one may be a little extravagant.

- **Voice-recognition telephone.** If your parent can't read the telephone keypad—even the large numbers—or has trouble finding numbers in the phone book, you might want to try a phone that works by voice recognition. Your parent says the person's name he or she wants to call, and the phone automatically dials the person's number programmed into the phone. (Programming is done by voice as well.)

- **Talking prescription recorder.** If your parent has a hard time reading the tiny type on prescription bottles, this device can help ensure he or she gets the right medicine at the right time. Just record (or have the pharmacist do it when the prescriptionis filled) the prescription number, date filled, the doctor's instructions, and what the drug is used for. Then attach the device to the prescription bottle and listen to the instructions when needed.

Other talking products include bathroom scales, thermometers and thermostats, VCRs, dictionaries, telephone caller ID, and even a talking tape measure. For more information on how to order these and other devices for low vision, and where you can learn more about vision problems and their treatments, see Appendix 2 in the Resources section at the back of this book.

Hearing Problems

Think of all you would miss if *you* had problems hearing—the sound of birds chirping, your favorite singer crooning, and your family and friends speaking. If your parent is severely hearing impaired, he or she probably misses those things too. Your parent may also miss important phone calls, instructions from the doctor, or the sound of a smoke alarm warning that there's a fire in the house. In other words, hearing loss can not only make life less pleasant, it can make it hard—even dangerous—for your parent to live independently.

Just like vision, hearing often deteriorates with age. At least one-third of all older adults experience age-related hearing loss called *presbycusis*. Subtle hearing loss may begin as early as our twenties and get progressively worse with each decade.

Age-related hearing loss generally results from the deterioration of nerve fibers in the inner ear, which enable us to perceive sound. High blood pressure or atherosclerosis (hardening of the arteries) can also cause or contribute to the problem, as can excessive exposure to loud noises over a lifetime.

For older people, hearing aids can help overcome some of the problems of hearing loss—if they are willing to wear them. Hearing aids work like a personalized amplifier, helping your parents hear sounds louder and more clearly. The devices work through three main components:

- A **microphone,** which picks up sound waves from the air and transforms them into an electrical current.
- An **amplifier,** which amplifies this current.
- A **receiver,** which converts the amplified current into a sound of greater intensity than the original.

Although the original hearing aids were large and cumbersome, modern technology has produced smaller and smaller devices, which are scarcely noticeable.

In addition to hearing aids, there are many other products that can help people with hearing impairments carry out their normal daily activities. There are also many things you as a caregiver can do. For both tips and products to help your parent, read on.

Five Tips to Cope with Impaired Hearing

1. **Speak slowly and clearly.** After the umpteenth "huh?" you may be tempted to shout what you have to say, but instead of increasing your volume, slow down and work on your enunciation.

2. **Meet them head-on.** People who don't hear well often compensate by learning to read lips. Your parent is more likely to understand what you are saying if he or she can see you talking. Avoid turning your back to your parent when you speak and keep your hands away from your mouth. If you have children, advise them to do the same when speaking to their grandparents.

3. **Avoid crowds.** Even if your mother can hear you well in a quiet room, she may not be able to hear you over the din in a crowded restaurant, particularly if she wears a hearing aid. If you'd like to have a conversation, a quiet place will be more pleasant for both of you.

4. **Amplify.** If your parent can't hear soft sounds, look for ways to turn up the volume. TVs and radios, of course, have volume switches. So do hearing aids. If your parent has trouble hearing callers, special amplifying devices can be attached to the telephone earpiece. Phone amplifying devices are portable. The same one that helps your mom hear callers on her home phone may be used on phones in hospital or hotel rooms or the homes of friends or relatives she visits.

5. **Rely on light and motion.** If your parent is hearing impaired to the point that he or she can't hear the doorbell, smoke alarm, or ringing alarm clock, look for modified devices that rely on light and motion, such as door chimes that light up instead of chime, smoke alarms with strobe lights, and alarm

clocks that can be placed under the pillow and set to vibrate at wake-up time.

Products for Low Hearing

Following are some of my favorite products and devices for adults with low hearing. You can find these at some medical supply stores or online at:

www.heartoday.com,
www.totalliving.com
www.hearmore.com.

• **Closed-caption TVs.** If your parent can't hear what is being said on television, perhaps he or she can read what is being said—kind of like watching a foreign film with subtitles. All new TVs have this capability. Using the TV's menu options, accessible by its remote control, you can activate and deactivate this feature in less than a minute. If your parent has an older TV without this capability, consider buying an external decoder, which hooks into the TV's cable line. Or better yet, buy a new TV with a bigger screen *and* closed captioning.

• **Flashing doorbell.** Does your parent often miss visitors or delivery people because he or she can't hear the doorbell? Try a doorbell that flashes instead of chimes. You can purchase receivers for each room of the house or apartment or purchase one portable unit that can be carried from room to room.

• **Phone amplifiers.** If your parent has a hard time carrying on phone conversations, an amplifier for the earpiece can help him or her hear callers better. If your parent sometimes misses a ringing phone, try turning the ringer on high or even purchasing a device that alerts via a TV screen that some-one—and who that someone is—is calling. Another option is a cordless phone, which your parent can carry from room to room. You parent is more likely to hear a phone ringing on the couch where he or she is sitting than in the next room.

• **Vibrating alarm clocks.** If a traditional alarm clock isn't loud enough to wake your parent from a sound sleep, try an alarm clock that can be set to vibrate and then be placed under the pillow. If a louder alarm would help, try a clock radio turned to a favorite radio station and then turn up the volume. Another option: Combine the two. One of my favorite products is the Sonic Boom Alarm Clock with Bed Shaker (www.goldviolin.com). Need I say more? If you have hard-to-wake teenagers, this product is guaranteed to get them up too!

• **Strobe smoke alarms.** We all know that smoke alarms save lives. But the traditional kind—the ones that emit an audible alert—won't work if your parent can't hear them. A better option: a smoke alarm with a flashing strobe light. Like traditional alarms, these go off when smoke is detected, but the audible alarm is accompanied by a bright strobe light. For nighttime protection, some models have a small unit that is placed under the pillow and vibrates if the alarm is set off.

For more information on how to order these and other devices for low hearing, and where you can learn more about hearing problems and their treatments, see Appendix 2 in the Resources section at the back of this book.

Balance and Mobility Problems

Whether they have pain and stiffness from arthritis in their knees or hips, fatigue and shortness of breath from congestive heart failure or emphysema, or some other debilitating problems, most older people don't get around as well as they used to. Changing vision, inner ear problems, certain medications, and aging muscles can lead to balance problems, which can make your parent less steady and more prone to falls.

For an older person, even a minor fall can be devastating. That's because aging bones become more porous and brittle. A fall that might barely leave a bruise on your buttocks could cause an elderly person to break a hip.

Older people who fracture a hip are up to 20 percent more likely to die in the year following their fracture than other people in their age group. Among those who live independently before the fracture, 15 to 25 percent will still be recovering in a long-term care institute a year after the fracture occurred.

Ten Tips to Help Prevent Falls

Obviously, to keep your parent independent, you must help him or her find ways to get around more easily while reducing the risk of falls. Here are ten tips to help reduce your parent's risk of falling. To find some the products mentioned, visit the following Web sites:

www.searsshowplace.com
www.drleonards.com
www.grabbarsonline.com
www.grabbars.com
www.arthritis.org
www.brucemedical.com
www.walkingcaneworld.com

1. **Improve balance.** Consult your parent's doctor or physical therapist about exercises he or she can do to improve balance, then encourage him or her to do them regularly. (See box on page 141 for a few sample exercises your parent can practice.)

One type of exercise you might want to try is tai chi. A study published in the *Journal of the American Medical Association* showed that practicing this gentle martial art improved the balance of the elderly and reduced the risk of falling. In fact, among several types of exercise studied, tai chi was the most beneficial, reducing falls and resulting injuries by 25 percent. An added benefit: Tai chi has also been shown to lower blood pressure and improve heart function in older adults. Many senior and community centers offer tai chi classes.

Also, don't forget to ask your parent's doctor or pharmacist about any medications he or she may be taking that could affect balance and whether there are alternatives to these medications.

2. **Eliminate clutter.** Shoes left at the top of stairs, a newspaper at the doorstep, a cat toy, or throw a rug on the kitchen floor. Any of these is an accident just waiting to happen. Tripping accidents are all too common in older adults. One way to help eliminate them is to get rid of clutter.

3. **Choose proper footwear.** Supportive, low-heeled shoes are best. Avoid athletic shoes with thick soles and deep tread, which can "catch" on surfaces and lead to falls. Have your parent toss any shoes with slippery soles and advise him or her not to walk in socks or stockings (the socks with treads you get in the hospital are fine), particularly if the home has polished wood or tile floors. If your parent wears shoes with laces, remind him or her her to always keep them tied or re-

place them with elastic laces that turn lace-up shoes into slip-ons—no tying needed!

4. **Light the way.** Make sure stairways, hallways, and rooms in your parent's home are well lit so your parent can see where

Three Exercises for Better Balance

Here are some exercises you can share with your parent. In fact, why not do them *with* your parent? You get the benefits of the exercises (it's never too early to start) and your parent doesn't have to do them alone.

1) *One-leg stands.* While holding on to a table, sofa back, or some other heavy, steady object, practice standing on one foot and then the other. Gradually increase the time you spend standing on each foot. Now let go and try standing on one foot.

2) *Heel and toe rock.* While holding on to your steady object, practice standing on your toes to a count of ten and then rock back onto your heels to a count of ten. Repeat several times daily.

3) *Hip circles.* While holding on to your steady object, make a big circle to the left with your hips, keeping your shoulders and feet steady. Now circle to the right. Repeat five times.

Source: Tinetti, M.; et al. "Reducing the Risk of Falls Among Older Adults in the Community." Yale *FICSIT* (1994).

he or she is going. For nighttime trips to the bathroom, you can even install a special light made just for the toilet seat.

5. **Use skid-proof rugs.** Reduce the risk of tripping accidents with rubber-backed rugs, or try adding a nonslip surface to the bottom of any rug (or secure them with double-sided tape). One product I have found useful is Rug Grippers®. Made with double-sided adhesive, these rug backings can be cut to fit any size or shape of rug and won't cause damage to the floor below.

6. **Make the bathroom safe.** Use a rubber bath mat in the shower or tub. Use a nonskid rug beside it. If your parent finds it difficult to walk or stand for long periods of time, have grab bars installed in the shower and beside the toilet and purchase a shower seat that will allow him or her to shower without standing.

7. **Get organized.** Have someone organize your parent's home (or do it yourself if you're feeling ambitious) so that most frequently used items are between waist and shoulder level. Often, falls occur when older people climb on stools, books, or stepladders to get to hard-to-reach items. Using a long-handled reacher can enable your parent to retrieve items from high shelves without climbing.

8. **Practice stair safety.** Make sure there are handrails on either side of the stairs, that the stairs are not slippery, and that the stairwell is well lit. Consider putting fluorescent tape on the edges of the top and bottom steps. If possible, move your parent's bedroom (if it's upstairs) and all frequently used items to the main floor of the house, thus minimizing the need to climb stairs and the risks associated with it.

The Right Way to Fall

While better balance and commonsense tips can prevent many falls, some risk still exists. But helping your parent learn the right way to fall—before it happens—can make the difference between getting up and walking away and being laid up indefinitely. The National Osteoporosis Foundation offers these tips to reduce the force of a fall, thereby lessening the risk of a broken bone.

• Show your parent how to fall forward or land on his or her buttocks. Falling sideways or straight down is more likely to lead to a hip fracture than falling in other directions.

• Tell your parent, if it's possible, that he or she should land on their hands or use objects around them to break a fall.

• Also, speak to your parent's doctor about whether he or she is a good candidate for padded undergarments that absorb the shock of a fall.

Source: Falls & Related Fractures published by the *National Osteoporosis Foundation*

9. **Use canes or walkers.** Though using a cane or walker is an obvious way to make their "steps" steadier, many older people hesitate to use them because of vanity. If your parent needs a cane to keep steady, strongly encourage him or her to use it. Many fashion-conscious women don't mind using a cane if it's attractive. Decorate a cane with fabric or ribbon to add flair (some women have several canes to match differ-

ent outfits) or purchase a Lucite® cane that can be filled with seashells, beads, or even colorful candies. At the least, insist that your parent carry a folding cane while out. (There's sure to be one that will fit in your mother's purse.) If your parent starts to feel unsteady, chances are he or she will be glad to have it and use it.

10. **Take advantage of delivery services.** Look for pharmacies and grocery services that deliver, and have your parent take advantage of them—especially when the weather is bad and sidewalks are slick. Ask the mail carrier to deliver directly to the door and the newspaper carrier to leave the paper on the front porch. One step onto an icy sidewalk or driveway can mean serious trouble for an older person with fragile bones.

Five Steps to Keeping Bones Strong

Although the focus of this section is on mobility and preventing falls, I think it's important here to briefly discuss bone health. That's because the weaker bones are, the more likely they are to fracture. In fact, for women with severe osteoporosis, merely coughing or lifting a pan from the oven is often enough to fracture a rib. Vertebrae, the bones that make up the back, can crumble and cause pain, with or without trauma.

Obviously, keeping your parent's bones as strong as possible will reduce the risk of fractures even if he or she does fall and, thus, help maintain independence. Here are five measures that can help.

EXERCISE

Like muscles, bones become weaker when you are inactive. Encourage your parent to be as active as he or she is able. Weight-bearing exercises (those in which the weight of the body is borne by the bones in the legs), such as walking or low-impact aerobics, are best for bones. But exercises that strengthen the leg muscles and promote balance are also important.

CALCIUM

If your parent is over sixty-five, he or she should be consuming at least 1,500 mg of calcium per day—the amount in about five cups of milk. Because it's rare for anyone (aside from babies) to drink that much milk, it's important for your parent to know about other sources of calcium such as yogurt, cheese, and other dairy products; fortified juices; whole almonds; and leafy green vegetables. It's also a good idea to make sure your parent takes a calcium supplement. Calcium comes in many different (and, often tasty) forms, including fruit-flavored tablets and chewy chocolate squares. While we're on the subject of calcium, I encourage you to increase your calcium intake too—even if you're still many years from old age. By the time you reach your mid-thirties your body starts to lose bone mass faster than it can build it, so it's never too soon to start caring for your own bones.

For foods that are good sources of calcium, see the Food Sources of Calcium chart on page 146.

VITAMIN D

For your body to use calcium properly, it needs adequate amounts of vitamin D. The exact amount varies depending upon age. The Food and Nutrition Board of the National Institute of Medicine recommends 400 international units (IUs) daily for people ages fifty-one to seventy and 600 IUs for people age seventy and over.

✐ Food Sources of Calcium

Food/Drink	Serving size	Calcium content (in milligrams)
Almonds	½ cup	200
Baked beans	1 cup	163
Broccoli (cooked, fresh)	1 cup	136
Cheese, cheddar	1 ounce	204
Macaroni and cheese	½ cup	180 (approximate)
Milk (whole, 2%, or skim)	1 cup	300
Orange juice (calcium fortified)	1 cup	300
Pizza	1 slice	220 (approximate)
Soy drink, (fortified)	1 cup	300
Spinach, (cooked)	½ cup	300
Tofu, (regular, processed)	⅓ cup	150
Yogurt, (plain)	1 cup	415

Normally, our bodies manufacture enough vitamin D in response to sunlight. But if your parent lives in the North, where the sun's rays are less direct, or if in a nursing home or is homebound, he or she probably needs a vitamin D supplement.

Vitamin D can also be found naturally in some foods including fatty fish, cod liver oil, and egg yolks and in fortified milk, cereal, margarine, and butter.

HORMONES

If you keep up with women's health news, you're well aware of the controversy surrounding hormone replacement therapy (HRT). Hormone replacement therapy helps restore levels of estrogen that protect women's bones prior to menopause, and it can help the bones of even very elderly women. But there are also some potential risks to taking HRT, so it's not appropriate for all women (nor is it appropriate for men). If you or your mother is interested, speak with a trusted doctor or other health-care professional and learn all you can before making the decision.

OTHER MEDICATIONS

In recent years, numerous drugs have been developed to strengthen porous bones. Unlike estrogen, many of these are appropriate for both men and women. They may also be appropriate for women who have been advised not to take estrogen for medical reasons. If porous bones are a concern, ask your parent's doctor about the following:

- Alendronate (Fosamax®)
- Calcitonin (Miacalcin®)
- Raloxifene hydrochloride (Evista®)
- Risedronate sodium (Actonel®)
- Teriparatide (Forteo®)

For more information on where to find aids for mobility and information on osteoporosis, see Appendix 2 in the Resources section at the back of this book.

Gripping and Dexterity Problems

As we reach middle age and beyond, most of us have some degree of osteoarthritis (OA)—pain and stiffness of the joints caused by the breakdown of cartilage that normally cushions our joints. While OA, often referred to as simply "arthritis," can affect almost any joint, for many people, the joints of the hands are hit hardest. As a result, gripping, grabbing, and holding objects with one's hands can be difficult.

OA of the hands and other problems, including strokes and neuropathy (nerve damage), can affect your parent's ability to do many normal activities like dressing, combing hair, preparing foods, doing craft projects, or playing cards.

Fortunately, as the population ages, many companies are creating products especially for people with gripping problems. Even more are taking dexterity into account when designing products for all of us. This is not only helpful for our older parents—it's also nice for all of us who enjoy the products' easy handling and stylish looks.

Twenty Tips for Less-Than-Nimble Hands

There are many simple and low-cost modifications you and your parent can do to make many tasks easier on sore, stiff, or less-than-nimble hands. Try some of the following tips, then check out the helpful products in "Get a Grip—Products for People with Dexterity Problems" beginning on page 154.

1. **Get rid of buttons.** If your parent has trouble buttoning clothing, encourage him or her to look for clothes that pull over, pull up, or zip. For blouses and shirts that button, try this tip: Remove (or find a seamstress who can do it) the but-

tons and sew up the buttonholes. Then sew the button over the buttonhole so that it shows on the front of the garment. Finally, sew Velcro® squares beneath the buttons. That way, the shirt always looks buttoned when your parent wears it. Only he or she knows how simple it is to open and close. To make zippers easier to zip, place a thin loop of fabric or yarn through the hole and tie the two ends together. Your parent can pull the zipper by placing a finger through the loop, eliminating the need to grip the tiny metal zipper. If your parent is in a hurry to get dressed and you don't have a loop of string handy, try a large safety pin in a pinch.

2. **Build it up.** In order to make handles of products easy to hold, build them up with materials you have on hand. Electrical or adhesive tape may work for the handles of hairbrushes, pots and pans, and small gardening tools. Those sponge curlers you may have used when you were younger work great over the handles of silverware, toothbrushes, small paintbrushes, pencils, etc. You can also purchase pipe tubing from your local hardware store. The material will slide easily over any utensils or items that have a handle, making the handle easier to grip. It will also help prevent the item from slipping out of your parent's hands if it is wet.

3. **Help your parent use the strongest muscles.** If your parent has difficulty opening drawers, cabinets, or even the refrigerator door, try placing fabric loops through drawer pulls and door handles. When your parent is ready to open, he or she can place a hand and arm through the loop and pull with the forearm.

4. **Use lightweight dishes.** The stoneware your mother got as an anniversary gift may be a little hard to lift and carry now.

Help save her hand joints by getting her some lightweight dishes—plastic works great and won't break if it's dropped. Better yet, encourage the use of sturdy paper plates for most meals. That way, your parent will be spared the cleanup too. Paper plates come in attractive designs appropriate for all occasions and décor.

5. **Look for texture.** When shopping for glassware or items with handles, look for texture. Bumpy, ridged, rough, or rubberized surfaces are usually easier to grip than slick ones. The same items can be useful, for you as well, to prevent slipping and breaking if your hands are wet or you have just used lotion.

6. **Pick easy-open bottles.** If there are no children in the home, forego the childproof prescription bottles, which can be hard on stiff hands. Ask the pharmacist to put prescriptions in easy-to-open containers or transfer them yourself to a medication dispenser. (Note: If children visit, of course, put medications where they can't be reached by small hands.)

7. **Spare the fingers.** If typing or pressing the buttons on a phone or microwave is difficult, suggest your parent use the eraser end of a pencil to do the job. If your parent uses a computer for e-mail or letter-writing, voice-recognition software can enable him or her to compose copy without having to key it in.

8. **Open up.** If your parent has difficulty opening plastic or cellophane packages such as the kind crackers, cereal, or sandwich meats come in, open the packages yourself and transfer the contents into "zipable" plastic bags or plastic containers that your parent can open and close easily when he or she is ready to use the product. For pretzels or chips, open the bag, fold down, and close with a chip clip available at supermarkets and discount stores.

9. **Go topless.** Removing the top from spray deodorant, shaving cream, hair spray, and aerosol cleaning products such as bathroom cleaner or furniture polish can be difficult for anyone. If your parent uses these products, remove the tops and store the cans topless. Another option is to purchase non-aerosol products such as roll-on or stick deodorant, pump hair spray, or pretreated dusting or disinfectant wipes. (The latter prevents your parent from having to use the extra strength to push down a spray can button!)

10. **Think small.** Economy-size jugs of juice, boxes of laundry detergent, or bottles of dish liquid may cost less than getting the equivalent amount in several smaller containers, but when gripping is a problem, smaller packages may be a better idea. When shopping for your parent, look for small, easy-to-grip containers. If he or she insists on large packages to save money, transfer the contents to smaller containers when you get the groceries home.

11. **Get the key.** If your parent still drives but has trouble turning the key in the door lock and/or ignition, check into getting a larger key, possibly with a plastic gripping surface at the turning end. If your local hardware store doesn't have such keys in stock, ask about special ordering or inquire about getting one from your local car dealership. If all else fails, try building up the end of the key with heavy tape or have your parent try turning the key with an old-fashioned clothespin. Just insert the key in the ignition, slip the clothespin over the end of the key, grip, and turn.

12. **Pick the right purse.** If your mom likes to carry a purse (and how many women don't?) encourage her to opt for a shoulder bag instead of a handbag. Wearing a shoulder

strap over her head and across her chest will help evenly distribute the weight of the bag's contents, eliminating stress on one shoulder. It will also spare her fragile hands and leave them free to hold on to other items, from umbrellas to railings along staircases. Another bonus: A shoulder bag is less likely to be snatched, a possibility that concerns many seniors.

13. **Twist—don't shout.** If your parent has trouble twisting the lids of jars, place a rubber mat on the counter and have him or her place a jar on the mat when he or she wants to open it. Once the jar is secure from slipping on the mat, your parent can use a rubber jar opener to grip the jar lid and open it. Often the first twist—the one that breaks the vacuum seal—of a jar of spaghetti sauce, peanut butter, or instant coffee is the hardest. If you shop for your parent and he or she will be using a product soon, try doing the first turn yourself. Replace the top gently and place it in the refrigerator, but make sure the jar top is closed so the contents will remain fresh and won't easily spill if dropped.

14. **Stop chopping.** If your parent enjoys cooking but finds it difficult to slice, chop, grate, or dice like before, take advantage of the many preprepared items at your local supermarket. Grated cheeses and potatoes (for hash browns), precut and packaged salad greens, egg whites in a carton (without the shells or fat-laden yolks), and chopped (sometimes frozen) chicken or vegetables are some of the greatest inventions since sliced bread!

15. **Discover new uses for scissors.** If gripping a knife is difficult, have your parent try using a large pair of kitchen shears to cut pats of butter, snip salad greens, chop the tops off of celery stalks, and even slice a pizza. Make sure kitchen scis-

sors are kept separate from those used for other purposes and that they are washed well by hand or in the dishwasher like other kitchen utensils.

16. **Ask for paper bags.** When grocery shopping, have your parent request paper instead of plastic. Although those lightweight plastic bags with holes for handles sound like a great idea, I find myself trying to grasp five in each hand and by the time I make it from car to kitchen, my hands are sore. Many seniors with dexterity problems tell me they find it much easier to get one large paper bag with their purchases and then hold it close to their chest with their arms around it. If your parent finds a full paper bag too heavy, ask the clerk to fill sacks halfway then encourage him or her to carry them one by one to the kitchen instead of struggling with two or three bags at a time.

17. **Order carefully.** If you are taking your parent out to dinner and you know he or she has difficulty cutting steaks or chicken, holding big sandwiches, or twirling spaghetti over a fork, feel free to suggest easier to manage menu options. Some good choices: beef tips with gravy and stir-fry or bite-size pasta (instead of long strands). If your mother would really like a steak or chicken breast, ask the waitress if the chef could cut it into bite-size pieces before sending it out. That will save your mom the embarrassment of having you lean over her plate and cut it for her. Another idea: Have her bring along her favorite large-handled silverware in her purse and bring it out when the meal arrives.

18. **Know how to play the game.** If your parent enjoys card or board games and has trouble rolling dice, have him or her

place the dice in a cup, shake the cup, and then toss out the dice. If cards are hard to hold on to, a plain old hairbrush can help. Have your parent place the brush, bristle-side up, on the table and insert the cards between the bristles.

19. **Keep a gripper.** If your parent has difficulty gripping, one of the best items kept at all times is a round rubber jar gripper. Your parent will be amazed at all it can be used for—from picking up small items to opening doorknobs. You can find inexpensive rubber grippers at discount and kitchen stores. The one I use most frequently arrived free in the mail as advertising for a local real estate agent.

20. **Let the sun shine in.** Drapes and curtains make an attractive window treatment while keeping out the sun. But for people with dexterity problems, opening and closing drapes and blinds can be a pain. To make the job easier for your parents, try replacing heavy drapes with ones made of lighter fabrics or exchanging cords and pulleys with easier-to-hold wands. If your budget permits, you can even have an electrician wire your parents' drapes to be opened and closed with the flip of a switch.

Get a Grip—Products for People with Dexterity Problems

People with arthritis in their joints and other problems that impair dexterity and gripping can find a variety of helpful products at stores that sell stationery, hardware, and home-building supplies, electronics, medical supplies, and kitchen wares. You'll also find some helpful products on the following Web sites:

www.seniorssuperstores.com
www.oxo.com

www.comforthouse.com
www.organize-everything.com
www.alfi.com,
www.productsforseniors.com
www.annmorris.com

Here are some of my favorite products that you and your parent may want to try:

- **Touch lamps.** Available in a wide variety of sizes, styles, and prices, these lamps come on with just a light touch to the base—no fiddling with tiny knobs. Another option is to purchase inexpensive Easy Grip Lamp Switches®. The switches, a little smaller than a sink faucet knob, replace the tiny ones that come on the lamp.

- **Easy-to-grip kitchen products.** An array of kitchen products come in easy-to-grip styles. These products feature ergonomically designed handles and include cutlery, tea kettles, kitchen tongs, pizza wheels, measuring cups, bottle openers, meat thermometers, and many others.

- **Large-button telephones.** The same telephones that can help people with low vision offer easier dialing for people with arthritis in the joints in their fingers. If dialing is extremely difficult, consider a voice-recognition phone. Your parent simply says the name of the person he or she wants to call (names and phone numbers must be programmed in beforehand, of course) and the phone does the rest.

- **Levered door handles.** Pushing a lever with the palm of the hand is much easier for most seniors than gripping and turning a doorknob. If turning knobs is a problem, have knobs replaced with levers or purchase doorknob extension levers that can convert existing doorknobs into levers. Another product you might want to try is Knobbles Doorknob Twisters®, a soft thermoplastic sleeve with eighteen ridges that make gripping and turning doorknobs easier. (They're also useful on faucet handles, gearshifts, tool handles, and bottles with twist closures.) Knobs on kitchen and bathroom faucets can be replaced with a single-lever faucet.

• **Large playing cards.** Oversized playing cards that are easier to see may also be easier to hold. If your parent enjoys playing cards and has trouble holding or shuffling them, try a playing-card holder, available at many medical supply stores, or even a battery-operated card shuffler that does the hard work itself.

• **Electric and battery-operated products.** Spare your parent's hands by treating him or her to easy-to-use electrical or battery-operated devices. You're no doubt familiar with electric can openers and toothbrushes, but did you know that you can also buy battery-operated vegetable peelers, electric sifters, and jar openers too?

• **Zipper pulls and buttoners.** These simple, inexpensive devices make getting dressed easier. Decorative zipper pulls hook on to most existing zippers, providing an extension that's easy to grasp and pull. A buttoner is essentially a flexible wire or plastic loop attached to a handle. Your parent inserts the loop through the buttonhole, grasps the button, and then pulls the button back through the hole—much easier than fiddling with small buttons with stiff fingers.

• **Book stands.** These devices sit on any table or desk and support an open book or magazine upright for hands-free reading. Many types are available from basic models to a deluxe version that is lighted and features compartments in the base for a notepad and pencil.

For more information

On where to find products for people with limited dexterity and where you can learn more about arthritis or other problems that affect dexterity, see Appendix 2 in the Resources section at the back of this book. For more tips for less-than-nimble hands, check out the *Arthritis Foundation's Tips for Good Living with Arthritis* (May 2001).

Cognition and Memory Loss

"Now that I'm older, I believe in the hereafter. I know I'm here, but I can't remember what I'm after."
—*Anonymous*

By the time people reach their seventies and eighties, most begin to suffer from at least a slight decline in thinking skills, commonly referred to as dementia. Common symptoms of dementia include a gradual loss of memory, problems with reasoning or judgment, disorientation, difficulty in learning, loss of language skills, and decline in the ability to perform routine tasks. Dementia that progresses can affect the ability to live actively and independently.

For more than four million Americans, dementia is caused by Alzheimer's disease, a disease that destroys brain cells (usually gradually) until eventually the person dies. In a national survey, 19 million Americans said they had a family member with the disease and 37 million said they knew someone with Alzheimer's. By the middle of this century, an estimated 14 million Americans will have Alzheimer's disease. But Alzheimer's is not the only cause of dementia. Other causes include several other diseases (like Parkinson's and Huntington's disease), strokes, depression, drug interactions, and thyroid problems.

When "Thinking" Problems Actually Become a Problem

If your parent occasionally forgets a name or walks into a room to retrieve something but can't remember what, don't panic. You can probably chalk up such occurrences to aging—or simply being human. (After all, don't you sometimes do the same things?) Just forgetting where you laid your keys doesn't mean you have Alzheimer's.

While an occasional "senior moment" is no cause for alarm, severe or persistent memory problems—particularly if they are joined by other thinking problems or behavioral changes—require a medical evaluation. If caught and treated early, some causes of dementia can be reversed. Many others can be treated.

According to the Alzheimer's Association's Web site (www.alz.org), the following symptoms are warning signs that your parent could have Alzheimer's or progressive dementia. Though not all people with these symptoms do have Alzheimer's, if your parent is exhibiting any of these signs, you should have him or her see the doctor.

• **Memory Loss.** One of the most common early signs of dementia is loss of short-term memory. Your family member may permanently forget appointments, names, telephone numbers, and family members' birthdays. If forgetfulness becomes a problem, don't necessarily assume your loved one has Alzheimer's. Problems such as stress and depression can also affect short-term memory.

• **Difficulty Performing Familiar Tasks.** People with dementia often find it hard to complete familiar everyday tasks. For example, they may find themselves unable to prepare a recipe, load and run a dishwasher, or even button their clothes.

• **Problems with Language.** We all trip over our words at times, but a person with Alzheimer's disease may forget simple words or replace familiar words with unusual ones, making communication difficult.

• **Disorientation to Time and Place.** It's not unusual to sometimes forget the day of the week (particularly if you are on vacation or otherwise away from your normal routine) or where you're going. But people with Alzheimer's disease may not remember the day, month, or even the year. They may become lost on their own street, forget where they are and how they got there, and not know how to get back home.

• **Poor or Decreased Judgment.** People with progressive dementia may dress inappropriately for the weather, wearing an overcoat in July or a sleeveless top in the middle of January. They may also show poor judgment about money, giving away large amounts to telemarketers or buying items they don't need.

• **Problems with Abstract Thinking.** Balancing a checkbook may be hard when the task is more complicated than usual (for example, if your parent has a lot of outstanding checks or has forgotten to enter a deposit). Someone with Alzheimer's disease could completely forget what the numbers are and what needs to be done with them.

• **Misplacing Things.** Anyone can temporarily misplace a wallet or key, but for a person with Alzheimer's disease, misplaced items may show up in unusual places: jewelry in the freezer, a carton of milk in the linen closet, undergarments in the oven, or a bottle of mustard in the medicine cabinet.

• **Changes in Mood or Behavior.** People with Alzheimer's may become depressed, particularly if they are starting to realize and come to grips with the fact that something is definitely wrong. They may also show rapid mood swings—from calm to tears to anger—for no apparent reason.

• **Changes in Personality.** People's personalities ordinarily change somewhat with age, but a person with Alzheimer's disease can change a lot, becoming extremely confused, suspicious, fearful, or dependent on a particular family member.

• **Loss of Initiative.** People with Alzheimer's often become very passive, sleeping late into the day, watching the television for hours on end, or retreating to an easy chair when you tell them it's time to change clothes, bathe, or brush their teeth. They may avoid all activities—even ones they once loved.

Keeping the Mind Active

As a long-running advertising campaign reminds us, "*A mind is a terrible thing to waste.*" Although your parent's mind may not be as sharp as it was at age twenty, the more he or she uses it, in general, the better and longer it will serve him or her. The more you encourage your parent to use his or her mind, the better for both of you. Here are some tips that should help.

• **Keep reading.** When an older person who always enjoyed reading either starts reading less or stops reading altogether, some caregivers panic, believing their loved one has lost interest in life. Ask your parent why he or she stopped reading. As I mentioned earlier in the chapter, reading problems often result as vision deteriorates. But it's in your parent's best interest to read as long as he or she is able. As is the case for all of us, reading enables your parent to keep up with current events, learn new skills, expand knowledge and vocabulary, travel to far-off places while never leaving the couch, and, most of all, enjoy life.

• **Jog memories.** If your parent's memory of past events or even family members' names is sometimes fuzzy, give a gift that will help preserve those precious memories. A shadow box with treasured objects such as a wedding invitation, a favorite handkerchief, one of your first baby shoes, photographs, and other mementos can both look attractive on the wall and help your parent to recall happy times in life. An album of family photos with the names of the people in the photos printed underneath in large letters can help your parent recall family members. A CD or audiocassette of favorite songs from the big band era can transport your parent to a time when he or she was young and energetic.

• **Give a challenge.** A mystery or novel may challenge your parent's mind. So might a good book of brainteasers, word games, or crossword puzzles. Find something your parent enjoys and encourage him or her to do it. A woman I know gave her elderly mother a handheld electronic game. She's the only person I know over eighteen (besides my father!) who has one, but she loves it!

• **Get some great gadgets.** If your parent often loses the keys or has trouble remembering to take medications, a number of different devices can help. My favorites: A key ring that beeps when your parent claps (allowing him or her to follow the sound of the beep to the misplaced keys), a talking medication dispenser that reminds when it's time to take a pill, or a talking timer that allows him or her to record messages that automatically play at certain times of the day to remind when it's time to start dinner or turn on the TV to watch a favorite show. If your parent can operate an ATM, he or she can use technology. Taking advantage of that can make life easier for both of you.

• **Be patient.** When your parent struggles to recall a name or select the right word, try your best to be patient. Help him or her find the appropriate word if it seems to be appreciated. If your parent gets agitated, however, let him or her take time. Eventually, he or she will recall the word or simply move on. If your parent tends to tell you the same story or joke over and over, try not to cut him or her off or steal the punch line. Act like you're hearing that story for the first time, and remember—one day you'll be older too.

Products to Enhance Memory and Keep the Mind Active

Classic TV shows, photo albums, puzzle books, and beeping gadgets are all good for helping spur your parent's memory or keep him or her thinking. Here are some of my favorite products to keep minds active. You'll find them on Web sites, including:

www.seniorstore.com
www.jigsawjungle.com
www.justjigsaws.com
www.age-in-place.com

as well as at many hobby, craft, book, and toy stores.)

• **Classic TV tapes.** *Burns and Allen, I Love Lucy,* and *The Jack Benny Show* are all sure to tickle your parent's funny bone and have him or her thinking back to a simpler time in life.

• **Crossword puzzles and word-search books.** A good puzzle book can keep your parent thinking and entertained for hours. If your parent has vision problems, check for large-print puzzle books.

• **Jigsaw puzzles.** Nothing gives the mind and hands a work-out like trying to turn a box of tiny shapes and colors into a poster-sized picture. If your parent has low vision or dexterity problems, try a puzzle with large pieces.

• **Hobbies and crafts.** Whether it's stamp collecting, crocheting, or model-car building, hobbies and crafts can keep seniors' minds involved and active.

• **Books.** Regardless of your age, reading is a great mind-booster, which increases your vocabulary, improves your thinking skills, teaches you about new subjects, and takes you to places you might never go otherwise.

• **Gadgets that remind them.** If your parent is forgetful, the following may help: A key ring that beeps when your parent claps and leads him or her to her misplaced keys, a medication bottle that alarms when it's time to take a dose, and a talking timer that allows him or her to record messages and replay them at certain times of the day.

For more information on where you can learn about Alzheimer's and other causes of dementia and their treatment, see Appendix 2 in the Resources section in the back of this book.

Emotional Problems

Sometimes your parent's greatest obstacle to independence isn't a problem with eyes, ears, balance, dexterity, or memory—it's the state of mind.

Unfortunately, some older people seem to tire of living and overcoming the obstacles life throws their way. They may think, "I've raised my family and worked hard all my life—now I'm finished." Some elders ask for more help than they really need—believing that after a lifetime of caring for their families it's time for their families to take care of them. Others retreat from life rather than seeking or accepting help or admitting their frailties. None of these behaviors is healthy.

As I mentioned earlier, it's important to help your parents when they absolutely need it. But it is also important to let even the oldest people continue to care for themselves and about others and the world around them. Both research and conventional wisdom tell us that the people who stay active and involved fare best in the long run.

Overcoming Emotional Obstacles

If you suspect emotional obstacles are impeding your parent's independence, the following suggestions may help.

USE AN INDIRECT APPROACH

Some mature adults with failing hearing, mobility, or eyesight choose to retreat from the world rather than seek medical care or make other accommodations, such as wearing a hearing aid or purchasing books on tape. If this sounds like your parent, approaching him or her indirectly about the change in behavior is usually more effective than the direct approach. So in-

stead of firing off to your mother, "Why haven't you been reading the paper?" try something like, "Mom, I know how much
you like making stained glass. Did you happen to read that
piece in the *Times* about it?" When she says no, you might say
something like, "That's not like you; you love to read."

Easing slowly into the situation is a nonthreatening way to
open up the lines of communication; it will diminish your parent's defensiveness and get him or her to talk freely. The goal is
to empower your parent to describe what is different and get
everyone involved in problem solving. That's a far better solution than wrestling control and treating your parent like a
child—or simply doing for your parent all of the things he or
she no longer is. As for the newspaper article your mom missed:
If you think it's something she would really like, cut the article
out and give it to her.

SEEK COUNSELING

As we discussed in Chapter 3, depression is common among elders. Depression doesn't always manifest itself as intense sadness.
Often elders who are depressed lose interest in activities they
once enjoyed or have feelings of hopelessness, such as "I can't
[fill in the blank] the way I used to, why should I even try?" Depression, as you read earlier in this chapter, is also a potential
cause of memory loss. Fortunately, depression in the elderly, to
an extent, is almost always treatable with medication, psy-
chotherapy, or a combination of the two.

Many family physicians and general psychiatrists can treat
depression in older people. If you or your parent's doctor think
he or she needs specialized attention, ask the doctor to refer you
to a geriatric counselor or psychiatrist. You're likely to find
them in most larger cities or affiliated with university medical
centers.

For the names of geriatric psychiatrists in your area, check the Yellow Pages or call the American Association for Geriatric Psychiatry at (301) 654-7850. You can also find the Association on the Internet at www.aagpgpa.org.

BE A CHEERLEADER

Just as you praise your children for developing new skills, praise your parent when he or she tries a new device or makes steps toward independence. Without being patronizing or condescending, look for ways to reward and encourage progress. At gift-giving time, for example, consider gifts that will make life easier or more interesting—a phone with large push buttons, an address book already filled with family members' names and phone numbers, a blouse with Velcro® closures, a book of mazes or crossword puzzles, a clock radio to replace the old key-wound model.

ASK THE RIGHT QUESTIONS

Don't make assumptions about why your parent is behaving the way he or she is. For example, if you realize your mother is no longer cooking, don't assume she's given up her desire to eat nutritious meals. Maybe she's used to cooking for a big family and now that everyone's gone she doesn't want to cook for just herself. Maybe arthritis in her hands makes it hard for her to chop vegetables or to turn the knobs on the stove. Maybe her oven isn't working. In other words, until you ask, you won't truly know.

As your parent ages, he or she may be faced with many obstacles to independence. Whether those obstacles involve hearing, vision, getting around, or getting motivated to take care of himself or herself, there are many things you can do to help your parent—and in doing so, help yourself. With the right tools and a little ingenuity, you can help your parent be as independent as possible for life.

Six

HOW CAN I COPE WITH CAREGIVING AND A CAREER?

As anyone who's ever been a caregiver can attest, caregiving is one of the most demanding, time-consuming, and exhausting jobs a person can have. But for many women, caring for an older parent or other relative is not their only job. In addition to having their own homes and families to care for, more than two-thirds of today's caregivers also hold jobs outside the home.

If you are trying to juggle the demands of caring for an aging parent with those of a job and family, clearly you are not alone. But the knowledge that millions share your plight probably does little to ease the stress you're feeling. Managing caregiving and a career is challenging even under the best circumstances. You may find yourself completely exhausted from one job, just as it's time to start another. But for many women, the hardest aspect of managing caregiving and work is that the two jobs can't be neatly divided. When you're responsible for the care of an aging loved one, it becomes virtually impossible to keep your personal and business life separate.

Juggling It All

Does your mother's doctor see patients at night and on weekends? Do her health professionals return your calls before 8 A.M. and after 5 P.M.? Does your father wait till you return from work to have an emergency that requires your attention? After staying up all hours to tend to a sick parent, do you wake up early, refreshed, and ready to start a new workday? Hardly!

For most women, caregiving inevitably infringes on their work time. A popular study by MetLife Healthcare showed that nearly 60 percent of caregivers employed outside the home are tardy, leave work early, or take extended lunch breaks and regularly spend *at least* one hour a week of work time making personal phone calls related to caregiving. Many women have told me they feel guilty taking time from work to handle caregiving matters; similarly, they report feeling guilty to be working when they feel they should be providing even more care for their parent.

The effects of juggling caregiving and career can be potentially devastating to both your health and your finances. Managing a job and a loved one's care can push you to the limit, opening you up to stress-related health problems, accidents, and mistakes at work. Caregiving exacts an enormous toll on women in the workplace in terms of missed days and less-than-optimal work performance.

The MetLife study I mentioned earlier also showed that 11 percent of women take a leave of absence from work to handle responsibilities related to caring for an ill, elderly relative. But those, perhaps, are the lucky ones. Many caregivers have to leave their jobs permanently to care for a sick parent, which affects their health coverage, retirement benefits (including Social Security and Medicare), or worse: Families can sometimes go broke caring for a loved one. Caring for an elderly parent or parents costs workers an average of $659,000 over their lifetime. Of that, $567,000 is due to lost wages, $67,000 to retirement contributions, and $25,000 in Social Security benefits.

But working caregivers don't shoulder that financial burden alone. The businesses that employ them suffer financially too, and that, indirectly, may benefit you!

Caregiving's Cost to Business— and What It Means to You

A recent study calculated that caregiving employees cost American businesses as much as $29 billion annually. Costs borne by employers include the following:

• **Replacement costs.** Businesses must bear the cost of replacing employees who leave due to caregiving responsibilities. These costs include recruiting, hiring, and training new employees to fill vacated positions.

• **The cost of sick leave.** Most businesses offer paid sick leave, which employees may use to care for a sick parent. When sick leave is exhausted, employees often use Family and Medical Leave Act time. (For more on the Family Medical and Leave Act, see page 180.) While employers are not required to pay an employee for time taken under the Family and Medical Leave Act, they *are* required to keep the employee's position open for twelve weeks. This can mean paying the cost of temporary employees or suffering reduced productivity while the employee is on leave.

• **The cost of interruptions and low productivity.** Caregivers may spend a fair portion of some workdays making calls re-

---

✑ Caregiving in the Workplace

64 percent of caregivers work outside the home

64 percent use sick and/or vacation time for caregiving

49 percent of caregivers arrive late for work or leave early

87 percent make phone calls related to caregiver responsibilities from work

26 percent passed up transfer or relocation opportunities due to caregiving responsibilities

56 percent of caregivers developed health- or stress-related problems that affected productivity at work

19 percent left one or more jobs due to caregiving responsibilities

11 percent have taken a leave of absence for caregiving responsibilities

6 percent of caregivers have given up outside work entirely

4 percent retire early because of caregiving responsibilities

(Source: The MetLife Juggling Act Study, Brandeis University)

lated to their parents' care. Not only are employers paying caregivers for the time spent on the phone, but employees are generally less productive when their workday is frequently interrupted by phone calls. The stress of caregiving can lead to absenteeism as well. Stressed-out employees are also likely to use sick leave or to be late for work.

While the cost to businesses is high now, the expense will only rise over the next decade and beyond. Some 78 million baby boomers are turning fifty at the rate of one every eight seconds. Approximately 80 percent of them have at least one living parent. During the coming decade, as the last of the baby boomers turn fifty and their parents enter their seventies and eighties, the number of caregivers in the workforce—in fact, those in their peak earning years—will rise steadily.

So what does this mean for you? Obviously, employers are not going to stop hiring caregivers. If they did, they'd be in for big problems—namely, a lack of qualified employees for many essential positions. The real solution for employers is to offer benefits that will help caregiving employees manage their personal and professional roles more efficiently. Offering eldercare benefits would help businesses recruit top new employees and improve the retention and productivity of existing ones.

Fortunately, that's exactly what some forward-thinking companies are already doing.

The Workplace Solution

Some companies have found that even relatively small, inexpensive benefits can make a big difference to overstressed caregivers. One company, offers its caregiving employees free consultations with a gerontologist or eldercare consultant. Although the cost to the company is about one dollar per employee, the company estimates that every consultation saves them between one and five workdays lost to employees taking time off or spending work hours on the phone locating information and eldercare resources.

Other companies are finding that simple and relatively inexpensive services, such as providing toll-free calls to eldercare experts and structured access to Web sites listing local eldercare programs, provide a good return on their investment. What's more, employees report that talking with eldercare experts and having such resources available gives them a feeling of being in control and a peace of mind that allows them to focus on their work.

Although simple and inexpensive resources, naturally, are the most popular among employers, some employers are going a step further to provide more comprehensive approaches to help their employees cope with caring for elderly relatives. These approaches may include seminars, the opportunity to telecommute, financial subsidies for caregivers, or even long-term care insurance.

One woman I spoke with said her employer allows employees to donate their unused vacation and sick leave days to other employees who need time off due to illness or caregiving duties. Thanks to the flexibility of her employer and the generosity of her coworkers, she says, she was able to take off five weeks with full pay when her mother broke her hip.

A lot of times, people don't even know that these small but helpful benefits are available. If you're not sure about the benefits your employer offers, just ask either your company's human resources director or someone from the employee assistance department.

Employers Leading the Way

If you are looking for a new job, selecting a caregiver-friendly employer is essential. But don't limit your job search to employers that specifically say they provide eldercare benefits. Benefits targeted to working parents can sometimes be just as helpful for you.

Each year, *Working Mother* magazine publishes a list of the 100 Best Companies for Working Mothers. Although the list, as the name suggests, was developed to recognize "parent-friendly" businesses, many of the companies offer a variety of benefits that are also useful for caregivers of aging relatives. They include benefits for part-time employees, telecommuting (the ability to work at home), job sharing, and compressed workweeks. (In many cases, this means four ten-hour days instead of five eight-hour days.)

This list of the top one hundred companies, as well as information about the specific benefits they offer, is available in *Working Mother* magazine. To order a copy of the magazine, go online to www.workingmother.com or call (800) 925-0788.

Getting Your Employer on Board

Even if you don't work for one of *Working Mother*'s Top 100, there's still a fair chance your employer offers benefits that can help your caregiving efforts. Perhaps your company offers telecommuting options, flextime, or generous sick leave that sometimes can be used to care for ill family members as well.

Maybe it pays for counseling to help you cope with the stresses of caregiving, or allows you to dress casually and comfortably—a real plus if you find it hard to get up and out in the morning looking perfect or if you have to rush home to caregiving duties.

If your employer doesn't offer benefits, you may have to fight for them. Creating a coalition of caregivers within your company can help. That's what my friend Marla did. When she took on the care of her elderly mother, Marla was aware of at least three women at her workplace who were in similar situations. As she started speaking to more women at work about her situation, she identified more than a dozen who were caring for elderly parents and frustrated with the company's rigid work schedules and lack of support for caregivers. Ten of the women got together and wrote a letter to the business's human resources director, explaining their difficulties and suggesting several concrete steps the company could take to improve their work situations and productivity.

Six months later, representatives of the group were invited to serve on a committee on employee benefits. Today, two years after Marla's mission began, her employer has instituted flexible work schedules and has added three extra days of annual leave for employees who have been with the company for at least a year. "It's not everything we asked for—far from it," Marla told me. "But it's a really good start."

The Future of Family Caregiving

During recent years, congress and the administration have begun to address the challenges of today's caregivers. Several long-term coalitions made up of businesses, trade associations, and nonprofit organizations have been created to educate the public and to place long-term care on the agendas of political candidates.

In 2002, the U.S. Department of Health and Human Services awarded $128 million in grants to states under the National Family Caregiver Support Program. The grants will help states develop community-based services and programs to benefit family caregivers. Such services may include counseling, support groups, training, and respite services. For a list of state allocations, go to www.aoa.gov, click on "Elders and Family," then scroll down to "Caregivers."

Additionally, the assistant secretary on aging at the Department of Health and Human Services has initiated the concept of a caregiver's tax credit. Although the initial amount of the proposed tax credit was a mere $1,000 and legislation for the credit was not passed, it did draw attention to the caregivers' plight among both lawmakers and the public.

Despite recent initiatives, however, it doesn't appear that the government has plans or money to begin covering long-term care for the nonindigent population. To the contrary, with billions of federal dollars going to fight the war on terror and strengthen the economy, Medicare is *cutting* benefits.

So what's a caregiver to do? Your best bet for now is to get help where you can.

• **Fight for benefits from your employer.** Urge your employer to offer eldercare benefits and other perks that would be beneficial to all employees. Stress to them that doing so is more than an act of generosity and kindness to their employees; it's a sound investment in the company's—and our nation's—future.

• **Insist on help from your family.** Caregiving isn't a one-person job. You need support. Siblings, spouses, adult children, and other family members should accept some of the responsibility.

- **Contact your local Area Agency on Aging.** They can refer you to other helpful resources in your area. To find your local area on aging, check with the National Association of Area Agencies on Aging at (202) 296-8130 or online at www.n4a.org.

- **Contact your congressmen and state and U.S. representatives.** Let them know the challenges caregiving presents and urge them to introduce and/or support legislation that might lighten the load—at least financially—for you and others in your situation. To find out which representatives and congressmen represent your area, log on to www.house.gov or www.congress.org. For bills to watch and updates on legislation that will impact caregivers, log on to www.caregiver.org/newsletters/winter2003_update.htm. For the most recent legislation and policy press releases, check out the National Family Caregivers Association Web site, www.nfacares.org, or the Family Caregiver Alliance Web site, www.caregiver.org.

What You Can Do Now

Managing caregiving without going broke—while maintaining your sanity—requires patience, nerves of steel, and creativity. But it can be done. If you want to keep working as long as possible or you fear that caregiving tasks will eventually require you to give up your job—along with your income and benefits—here are five things you can do *now*.

Find Out What Your Employer Offers

Ask if your employer offers any type of employee assistance plan. If so, find out what's available and how to use it. If not, make a case for your employer to add benefits. (Keep in mind that benefits such as flextime, flexible spending accounts, job sharing, and even casual dress days are valuable to *all* employees, not just caregivers.) Use the statistics and other information in this chapter to help make your case.

Even if your employer doesn't offer or agree to provide eldercare benefits, there are things you can do in the workplace informally. I have talked to women who have formed networks of fellow caregivers to:

- Share information
- Meet for lunchtime support groups
- Cover for one another when one has to be off for caregiving duties.

Look Elsewhere

If you are looking to make a job move or career change, look into employers' benefits packages before you accept a job—better yet, before you even apply. Don't know where to start your job search? Check *Working Mother* magazine's 100 Best Companies for Working Mothers (see information on p. 175). But don't stop there.

Increasingly, businesses are finding that to recruit and retain good employees, they must offer more than a salary and two weeks of paid vacation. Even if the employer you're considering doesn't offer eldercare services directly, options such as job sharing, flextime, or paid vacation and insurance for part-time employees can help you keep your job (and benefits) while caring for your loved one. Consider any perks a prospective employer offers as part of your total compensation for the job. In many cases, you'll come out better in the long run by taking a job with a smaller salary but better benefits.

Look Ahead

If your parent doesn't need care now or needs only minimal care, don't assume that will always be the case. Sometimes, an older person's health takes a quick turn for the worse. At best, assume you will be providing more care—rather than less—as the months and years go on.

By looking ahead, you can start to consider future career options or sources of income to sustain you when and if you must give up your job. Contact a geriatric care manager or eldercare counselor who can help you think through possible care scenarios and inevitabilities before they arise from necessity. Consult a financial planner to help you figure out what assets you have to pay for care when you need it. Check into federal and state programs that help cover health-care costs (see Financial Resources on page 186) and find out which of your parent's medical costs are tax deductible or covered by insurance.

By knowing what to expect and where to find resources when you need them, you'll be better prepared to handle crises as they arise. If your employer offers an employee assistance plan, ask if the plan covers referrals to a geriatric care manager. If not, ask your parent's doctor for a referral or locate one by contacting the National Association of Professional Geriatric Care Managers at (520) 881-8008 or through the association's Web site, www.caremanager.org.

Some hospitals offer the services of geriatric care managers free of charge or for a small fee. If you must pay out-of-pocket, the cost of a consultation is well worth the hassle and heartache (not to mention missed time from work or hours on the phone at your desk). And you'll be helped if you were to have a crisis and didn't know where to turn for assistance.

If All Else Fails, Use Family and Medical Leave

You've used every minute of personal leave and sick leave you've accrued, and now your mother is going to the hospital for surgery. Will you have to quit your job to stay with her? Not necessarily. If the company you work for has at least fifty employees and meets other criteria, the federal government (under the Family and Medical Leave Act) requires them to allow you up to twelve weeks off a year to care for an ill family member. As I mentioned earlier, your employer is not required to pay you for your time (and few, if any, will). But they are required to continue your benefits and keep your position open during your absence.

Although most people assume Family and Medical Leave applies only if you need large chunks of time off, you can actually use it in increments as small as fifteen minutes. If you need to leave fifteen minutes early to pick up a prescription on the way home or must come in an hour late after taking your father to the doctor, consider charging it to your Family and Medical Leave. Although it's not the optimal situation—and you shouldn't use it if you have personal or sick leave available—it is an option worth considering if you might otherwise lose your job.

Be Mindful of Finances

Unless you are independently wealthy, giving up your job or forking over your paycheck to pay for your parent's care can be financially devastating. To make the most of the money you have now and help ensure a better future for yourself and your family, you may need to make some serious financial decisions and commitments.

If you don't already have a savings plan in place, now is the time to start one. If you have the option of paying into a retirement account—particularly if your employer matches contributions—make the largest contribution you are able to, even if it means making some sacrifices elsewhere. Depending on your parent's age and health, you may be able to take out a long-term care policy (some employers offer group rates). If your parent doesn't qualify or the premiums are too high, consider taking out one for yourself. By purchasing now, when you are relatively young and healthy, you may be able to get a policy that's affordable and will allow you to spare your own family some of the financial struggles you may be facing now.

Caring as a Career

If your parent has the assets to cover some type of care, but not necessarily the cost of a nursing home—or if you'd prefer to keep your parent in his or her own home but can't pay for the care that would require—you may be able to make caregiving your paid job.

That's what Sherry did. After her mother died, Sherry's father was left alone and unable to care for himself. Not wanting to send her father to a nursing home, Sherry left her job as a dental assistant and moved her husband and family into her father's home, where she cared for him for the next four years until he died. Sherry's brother, who managed their father's finances, paid Sherry $30,000 a year, a salary comparable to what she had made at the job she left, but considerably less than the annual cost of a nursing home.

Though the job was the hardest one Sherry has ever had—or likely will have—her father got the care he needed in his own home, and Sherry's salary (along with that of her husband, a sporting goods store manager) enabled the couple to raise their own two children without going bankrupt.

If you want to consider an arrangement like the one Sherry had and your parent doesn't have the funds, see if your state's Medicaid program allows elderly people needing round-the-clock nursing care to hire family caregivers to provide their care. (Some, but not all, do.) To find out if your state is one that offers this benefit, go to www.care-givers.com, www.aarp.org, or www.medicare.gov. There, you will find links and ways to search for information on your state's Medicaid and Medicare programs.

Regardless of how you are paid, be prepared for a long, hard road. While this type of arrangement may make it possible financially to care for your parent, it isn't a cure-all when it comes to balancing finances and family responsibilities.

Sherry, for example, found that leaving her paid job to care for her father meant giving up valued relationships with coworkers and the stimulation of working outside the home and seeing patients. Caregiving took a toll on her health and family life as well. While lifting her father up in bed one day, she suffered a back injury that left her laid up for a week and still bothers her occasionally. She also suffered problems in her marriage, had little time to spend with her growing children, and was taken advantage of by her siblings. "Once my brother and sister began to see me as the 'paid caregiver,' they became a lot less willing to take on caregiving tasks themselves," she told me.

Financially, the situation has its drawbacks too. Though you may draw a salary for providing care, you'll be giving up job benefits, including Social Security contributions and employer-sponsored retirement benefits. Depending on how long you have worked prior to becoming a caregiver, this could make a difference in whether or not and how much Social Security you will draw when you retire.

Letting the Consumer Choose the Care

Not long ago, care for low-income elders was limited largely to that provided by nonpaid family members, approved personal care agencies, county-run nursing homes, and other indigent-care facilities. But thanks to a movement called "consumer-directed care," options for low-income seniors (and their families) are improving.

One of the most progressive and highly publicized consumer-directed care programs is the "Cash & Counseling" (C&C) demonstration project. The project entails giving consumers supplemental income to spend, as they need, instead of a set of services prescribed by a case manager. Arkansas was the first state approved by the federal government to allow Medicaid clients a cash allowance to purchase services tailored to their exact needs; similar projects have been implemented in New Jersey, Florida, Texas, Oregon, and Colorado. Other states are likely to join their ranks soon.

Under the program, clients are able to choose and hire their own personal care aides and arrange services to suit their own schedules. Consumers can use their monthly cash allowances to hire family members, friends, or anyone else to provide care, or to buy equipment or devices to increase their independence.

The program offers benefits for all involved:

- **For seniors,** the program is empowering. The ability to choose providers, services, and equipment is expected to improve consumers' independence and quality of life. Seniors also have the opportunity to hire people they know, love, and trust to be their caregivers.

• **For caregivers,** the program offers the opportunity to be paid for tasks that might necessitate their giving up paid work. Another plus of the C&C project is that it applies family caregivers' wages toward their Social Security accounts. In other words, if you care for a relative under this program, your Social Security status doesn't suffer because you leave the traditional paid workforce. Your Social Security benefits continue to accrue. The program also provides training for family caregivers.

• **For policymakers,** C&C and other consumer-directed programs offer potential cost savings by naturally expanding the supply of caregivers to better meet the demand.

If you think you might like to provide care to your parent for a salary, broach the subject with family members, particularly the one responsible for your parent's finances. Explain that in most cases this is a less expensive option than a nursing home or outside care and one that your parent may be more comfortable with. If your family is receptive and you decide to accept the job, make sure it is treated like a "real" job. Get a written contract outlining what you are expected to do and how much you will be paid and when. Make sure the contract allows for regular vacations and respite care, reimbursement for any out-of-pocket expenses associated with your parent's care, and salary increases at least once a year. An elder-law attorney can help you draw up a contract. It's best if an attorney or an impartial third-party (not a family member) writes the paycheck.

To see if C&C or similar programs are available in your state, check out the following Web sites:

Consumer Direction
www.consumerdirection.org

University of Maryland—Center on Aging
www.hhp.umd.edu/AGING

U.S. Department of Health and Human Services
http://aspe.hhs.gov

✐ Financial Resources

If you are already paying for an elderly loved one's care or just planning for it, the following sources can help:

In the Book Store
• *Long-Term Care: Your Financial Planning Guide* by Phyllis R. Shelton (April 2003).

• *Alzheimer's Disease: Fighting for Financial Survival* by Edward D. Beasley, David H. Ferber, LLM (October 2000).

• *The Complete Idiot's Guide to Long-Term Care Planning* by Marilee Driscoll (August 2002).

• *The Unofficial Guide to Eldercare* by Christine A. Adamec (June 1999).

On the Web

• National Council on Aging Benefits Checkup
A free service to help older Americans and their families identify state and federal assistance programs.
www.benefitscheckup.org

• Costs of Caregiving
Site offering information on federal, state, and personal resources for covering health care costs as well as financing options and advice on managing the costs of caregiving.
www.costs-of-caregiving.com

• Help Guide
Site featuring noncommercial links for eldercare decisions and financing.
www.helpguide.org/elderfinancing.htm

• American Association of Retired Persons (AARP)
Offers information and free copies of publications on a wide range of eldercare issues, including long-term care and health-care financing.
www.aarp.org

Paying for Your Parent's Health Care— Without Going Broke

There's never a good time to take on the care of an elderly parent. But for many people, women especially, the timing—the peak of their careers, while putting children through college and saving for their own retirement—couldn't be worse.

If your family is wealthy, the cost of care probably isn't an issue; if your parent is indigent, Medicaid will at least cover the cost of a nursing home. But if your financial status is somewhere between the two extremes, cost can be an obstacle to getting your parent the care he or she needs. Paying for care can be financially devastating.

The following tips can help.

Cut Drug Costs

If your parent is on several medications, as many elderly people are, the cost of drugs may be one of the bigger (if not *the* biggest) monthly expenses. Sadly, many older people and their families have a difficult time paying for prescription drugs. I can't count the number of times I've heard older people say that they don't take all of the medications their doctors prescribe because they simply can't afford them. And a recent study confirms this trend. The Kaiser Family Foundation reported that, because of high drug costs, nearly one quarter of seniors were not filling prescriptions. I wonder how many older people have been put in nursing homes prematurely because they couldn't afford medications that would have helped them function. For seniors with very low incomes and assets, as well as those with more than $5,100 in annual drug costs, the Medicare Prescription Drug law passed in late 2003 offers a solution to getting more affordable—and in some cases, free— medications. For helpful articles on the specifics of the new legislation and how (or if) your parent might benefit, check out the AARP website (www.aarp.org). Hopefully, your parent doesn't have to forgo medications—and you don't have to go broke buying them. For additional solutions on how to save on medications, see "Six Tips to Make Medications Affordable" on page 193.

Minimize Other Expenses

Suppose you were saving for a down payment on a house or had decided to raise a family on one income. You'd probably look for ways to cut your expenses and minimize other expenditures. The same goes if you're trying to help pay for your parent's care.

If you consider your expenses carefully, you may find that you're spending more than you really need to on your morning cup of coffee at a trendy coffeehouse when you could brew your own inexpensively at home, on premium cable channels you rarely (if ever) watch, on payments for a luxury car when a more practical model would suit you just fine, or on wasted energy from setting your home's thermostats higher or lower than you really need to. These are just a few examples. Take a close look at your budget and keep a record of what you spend—and on what—over a four-month period. Unless you are already faithful to a budget, you may be surprised to see where your money goes.

Use Your Parent's Assets to Pay for Care

Just because your parent needs an expensive prescription filled, a taxi ride to the doctor's office, or grab bars installed in the shower doesn't mean that you, as the caregiver, have to pay for all of those things. One of the most underused sources of funds for such expenses may be your parent's own assets. Many of today's elders cling to a Depression-era mentality, feeling they must save every penny or do without tomorrow, and therefore may be more than willing to let you cover those costs. The fact is that many older people have ample assets to cover a lifetime of care. And as I mentioned earlier, in some cases it's possible to tap in to those assets to pay you or another family member to serve as a caregiver. What if the money does eventually run out? Only at that point does it become your responsibility to step in and help financially.

Tap in to Your Home's Equity

If you own a home, it is probably your biggest asset. In many cases, you can tap in to that asset by applying for a home equity loan (also called a second mortgage). Although mortgage interest rates are on the rise again after reaching forty-year lows last year, they're still lower than interest rates on most credit cards, consumer loans, and other sources of financing. What does this mean? It means that borrowing money will cost you less than if you borrowed from other sources—and you can probably borrow more too. Some lenders will let you borrow as much as 125 percent of your home's equity (the difference between your home's worth and how much you owe on it). In other words, if your home is worth $300,000 and you still owe $200,000 on it, you might be able to borrow up to $125,000 using your home as collateral.

If you can't bear the thought of possibly risking your home to pay eldercare costs, you may still benefit from refinancing your home. Most lenders say that if your current mortgage is at least two points higher than the current rate (for example, your mortgage is 10 percent and the current rate is 8 percent), you'll save money by refinancing if you plan to stay in your home long enough to off-set the actual costs of the refinancing (points, title insurance, etc.). Refinancing can not only reduce the amount of interest you pay, it may also allow you to stretch out your payments over more years, meaning individual payments are reduced, although you will ultimately pay more in interest if you choose to do this. Depending on the cost of your home and the difference in your previous and new interest rates, you may save as much as several hundred dollars each month. You can use that money, if necessary, to help pay eldercare expenses.

Before you decide to take out a second mortgage or refinance your home, consider the long-term financial implications of such a decision. Failure to repay a second mortgage in a timely way could cause you to lose your home. Refinancing could extend your mortgage payments well into your own retirement years. So consider your options carefully and choose wisely.

Check into Reverse Mortgages

Even if your parent is low on cash to pay for care, he or she may have the resources for long-term care in the home—literally. Depending on the area of the country and the exact city where your parent lives, a home that was purchased for $20,000 in the 1950s could be worth hundreds of thousands today.

An alternative to taking out a second mortgage on your home is to have your parent take a reverse mortgage. Unlike a traditional mortgage—in which you make payments to live in the house—a reverse mortgage pays you a lump sum or monthly payments while you live in the house. The payments, of course, depend on the value of the house, your parent's age (the older he or she is, generally, the more money will be received), and some other factors, but may be sufficient to pay for medical expenses, home repairs, or modifications, or some in-home care. While your parent will be able to remain in the house for the rest of his or her life under a reverse mortgage, the loan must be repaid—usually through the sale of the house—when he or she moves, sells the house, or dies. Therefore, a reverse mortgage is not an option for someone who wants to leave the home free and clear to any heirs.

If you think your parent might be interested in a reverse mortgage, speak with the bank, mortgage lender, accountant, and tax attorney. Be aware that some federal programs consider reverse mortgage payments to be "liquid assets" or income. These assets may affect eligibility for some government programs. A good source of general information about reverse mortgages is the AARP Web site, www.aarp.org.

Remember: This type of transaction is not for everyone. As with home refinancing, this may have long-term financial effects; if you are seriously interested in taking advantage of a reverse mortgage, make sure you do all of your homework before you make a final decision.

Have Your Kids Help Foot Their Own College Bills

Sure you want your child to go to a good college. But going to a good college doesn't necessarily mean going to the most expensive choice. Nor is there any rule that you have to be the one to pay for it. Perfectly good state colleges (as well as relatively inexpensive community colleges) abound, as do scholarships for students wanting to attend those more pricey universities. If your child is in high school now, have him or her speak with a guidance counselor about college choices and scholarships for which he or she might qualify. You can also search for sources of college funds on the Web. Here are few sites to get you started: www.fastweb.com, www.1stcollegescholarship.com, and www.realizethedreamfoundation.com. Other options include having your child work summers and after school to help cover tuition costs and applying for student loans, which your child can pay off once heor she is gainfully employed.

Although this is a highly personal issue that each family will have to consider carefully, I feel strongly that by having your child help defray the cost of his or her own education, you'll be doing everyone a favor—you will save money, and your child will appreciate education more if he or she has helped pay for it.

Check Tax Laws and Medical Spending Accounts

If you provide the majority of care for an older loved one, it may be possible to claim him or her as a dependent on your income tax. It may also be possible to deduct a portion of your parent'smedical expenses from your income tax. Check with your accountant. Also, some companies have flexible spending accounts whereby employees can save pretax dollars to pay medical-related expenses for themselves and immediate family members. If your employer offers this benefit, see if money you contribute can be used to pay for your parent's medical bills. Even if parents are not covered, contributing to a flexible spending account may help decrease your taxes. Incidentally, similar accounts can offer savings on child-care expenses while you work.

❖ Six Tips to Make Medications Affordable ❖

If medication costs are eating up your parent's income or he or she simply can't afford the needed medications, the following six tips can help.

1. *Contact patient assistance programs.* Almost all drug manufacturers have programs that offer free or discounted drugs to elderly people meeting certain income requirements. In fact, according to the Pharmaceutical Research and Manufacturers of America (PhRMA), 3.5 million seniors received free drugs from its member organizations in 2001. If you think your parent

might qualify for free drugs, ask the doctor to contact the drug's manufacturer.

2. *Ask for samples.* Pharmaceutical representatives often give doctors samples of drugs they are selling. Ask your parent's doctor if there are samples of the drugs your parent needs. Even a few weeks' worth of free medication is a good start, particularly if you are waiting to see if the drug helps or will be covered by an assistance program.

3. *Check into pharmacy cards.* Some drug companies offer discount cards for their own drugs. (Check with individual pharmaceutical companies about their cards.) In a few cases, pharmaceutical companies have joined forces to offer discounts to people who have difficulty paying for prescription drugs. For example, Together RX is a prescription savings program that offers a free, easy way to save approximately 20 to 40 percent on more than 170 medications manufactured by more than a half dozen companies. Though your parent will have to meet certain income requirements to qualify, those criteria are generally less stringent than for people applying to patient assistance programs.

4. *Look for group discounts.* If your parent is a veteran or a member of another group or organization, drug discounts may be part of the membership benefits. AARP, for example, offers its members savings of about 17 percent on brand-name drugs and about 50 to 55 percent on generics. You can search the AARP drug database to find your parent's medications and order them directly through the association at www.aarp.org.

5. *Inquire about drug chain discounts.* Many drugstore chains, including CVS and Walgreen's, offer discount cards for frequent buyers. Shoppers can use the cards to get discounts on selected items, and all purchases made by card users are recorded. When

purchases reach a certain dollar amount, the customer gets a coupon that can be used like cash to purchase items in the store.

6. *Find out what your state offers*. More than thirty states have instituted programs that provide some form of assistance to older and disabled citizens who lack drug coverage. These programs differ substantially from state to state. Some are targeted to lower income beneficiaries, while others extend up to more moderate-income levels. Some provide unlimited benefits, while others impose annual benefit caps on enrollees or restrict coverage to certain classes of drugs. Some offer direct benefits, while others seek only to reduce prices. Regardless of the type of benefits your state may offer, these programs are worth checking in to. To find out what your state program offers, log on to www.medicare.gov and click on the link for Prescription Drug Assistance programs.

Seven

WILL I EVER GET
MY LIFE BACK?

Does your world revolve around transporting your loved one to appointments, picking up prescriptions, placing calls to doctors (and then waiting for return calls), checking out long-term care options, and hiring and managing home health aides? Does your head spin with the responsibilities of caregiving? Does your world feel out of control? Sometimes, when you have a moment to think, do you wonder, "Will I ever get my life back?"

The answer to your question, in part, is no—you can never get back the life you once had. Life will never be as carefree as it was when your parent was the one taking care of you. Life will never be as easy as it was in your younger adult years when it seemed youth and good health—both your own and your parent's—would last forever. The good news, however, is that you can have a really great, fulfilling life, though you may have to work a little harder at it. In fact, in the days of caregiving and beyond, you can build a life that is more rewarding, more enjoyable, and more exciting than when you may have taken loved ones, good health, and life itself for granted.

It's often in times of loss that we most appreciate what we have left. When hardships hit, we become more resilient. When we feel down and lonely, we seek out new friendships. When we wonder where life is leading us, we make steps to chart our own destiny.

Be grateful for the time and opportunity you have to provide for your parent. At the same time, don't lose sight of yourself and your own needs, hopes, and dreams. While you are busy caring for your parent, who is taking care of you? Probably no one, unless you do it yourself.

I have talked to many women over the years who gave their lives to caregiving and then woke up one day to find life had passed them by. Many have told me they've neglected jobs, marriages, friendships, and relationships with their own children to fulfill their caregiving duties. Others have told me they feel tired and haggard or are suffering health problems from years of neglecting their own health. Don't let this happen to you. *The best time to get your life back is before you completely lose it!*

While many women throw themselves into caregiving because it has to be done and there's no one else to do it, I'm convinced there are others who use caregiving as an excuse for putting their dreams on hold or as a way to avoid risks. Regardless of what may be holding you back, I urge you to stop waiting for the right opportunity to pursue your dreams. If you wait for the perfect time, that time will never come.

In the previous chapters you learned some ways—and reasons—to free up more time for yourself. Use this time to your advantage. Search your heart and mind for what makes you happy, try new things, take risks, consider what would give you satisfaction both now and in the long run—and then do it! In this chapter, I'll tell you some ways to nurture both your body and soul and, yes, to get a life you love.

Seek out Excitement

Are you caught in a rut with your caregiving? Do you feel like you'd do anything for a break? Do you remember how it felt to be a kid with no worries or responsibilities? What you need is a little excitement.

At fifty-eight, Caroline is a full-time caregiver for her father who has amyotrophic lateral sclerosis (ALS), which has left him virtually paralyzed. Though she rarely leaves her father for more than an hour at a time, her grown daughter comes occasionally to give her some respite. One summer morning when Caroline *really* needed some respite, she called her daughter Amy to see if she might be available to come by for a few hours. "I would love to," her daughter told her, "but I promised to help chaperone Nick's [her son] Cub Scouts' trip to Six Flags today."

"Then how about we trade places for a day?" Caroline asked. The offer surprised Amy. Amusement-park rides scared her mother, and an afternoon with a group of nine-year-olds hardly sounded relaxing. But Caroline sounded desperate for a break of any kind, so Amy agreed.

Later that day, as Caroline walked through the hot amusement park with her charges, a few of the boys suggested she ride the log flume with them. Though the thought of any ride didn't appeal to Caroline, this one seemed tame compared to others. After a short wait in line, the children and Caroline boarded the big artificial log and prepared for the descent. Then the unexpected happened: Caroline had fun. So much fun, in fact, that she suggested they ride again. When the next ride went well, she agreed to try something a little more adventurous—a roller coaster.

For the rest of the afternoon, Caroline enjoyed the rides as much as the boys did. She had so much fun that she offered to take her grandson Nick back—just the two of them—later in the summer, when they could ride every roller coaster in the park at least twice.

Though an enjoyable day at an amusement park may seem like a small thing, for Caroline it was a turning point in her life. Since becoming so involved in the care of her father, she had forgotten how to have fun. What's more, she found fun in an unexpected place—on amusement-park rides that once terrified her. Strangely, she told me, the afternoon with her young grandson gave her a new kind of courage. At fifty-eight, she was able for the first time to ride a roller coaster. Maybe she could make it through this caregiving thing too.

If you too feel like you have forgotten how to have fun, now is the time to go out and rediscover it. If you're not sure how, take cues from your child or grandchild. If you don't have children of your own, observe—or even borrow—a friend's child. Fun comes naturally to children.

If you have a fear that you've never quite conquered, now may be the time to do that too. Like taking that first roller-coaster ride, conquering a fear can be both liberating and inspirational. Angie was once so afraid of heights that she felt sick to her stomach just riding up an elevator or looking out a second-story window. She overcame her fear by bungee jumping. "Once I paid my money and took the frightening elevator ride to the point where I was supposed to jump, I was almost as afraid of backing out as I was of jumping," she said. The man who took Angie up in the elevator told her to start counting to three as soon as she stepped off the platform. By the time she reached three, he said, she would be safely dangling in the air. "Three seconds," she thought, "I can handle three seconds of fear." So she made the jump and had the time of her life!

I have heard several stories of women who were afraid of flying or falling and who faced their fears by skydiving. One woman who was afraid of speaking in front of people took a public speaking class at her local community college. Another, who was ashamed of her ample figure and usually hid it under baggy clothes, took a belly-dancing class.

When you care for someone (or perhaps several someones) day in and day out, it's easy to neglect your own need for fun or to play it safe in the confines of your home and routine activities. Don't feel guilty about getting out now and then. Try something outrageous. Try something daring. You'll never know what's waiting for you until you try.

Find a Hobby

Is there something you love to do or have always wanted to do but couldn't find the time? Or have your caregiving responsibilities taken you from activities you once loved, leaving your life with a void? Why not start a new hobby or revisit an old one? Believe it or not, now may be the best time to start making, doing, or collecting. It may be just the one thing that will keep you sane. Though starting a hobby may seem out of the question at this time of your life, I know of several caregivers who have done it.

As a child, Mary was always a tomboy. Though her mother and grandmother tried to teach her to knit and do needlework, Mary was never interested. Her knitting always came out a mess, and trying to cross-stitch made *her* cross. She preferred to run, play ball, and climb trees with the neighborhood boys. What she enjoyed most, however, was watching her grand-father whittle, as he called it. As an adult, Mary fondly recalled her grandfather sitting on his wide front porch carving toys from blocks of wood, bars of soap, or practically anything he could find to cut into. She especially loved the zoo animals he carved for her. They have remained some of her most treasured possessions.

As Mary's mother grew older, Mary found herself doing more and more to help her. The new responsibilities cut into the time she had to enjoy outdoor activities, which had once occupied almost all of her leisure time. Although she used to spend off-hours and weekends camping and hiking with her family and coaching her teenage daughter's softball team, Mary had begun spending increasing amounts of time just waiting—for her mother's doctor to call her back to the examining room, for physical therapy appointments to begin, for tests to be completed, for health-care professionals to come to the phone or return her phone calls. Always one to be active, the waiting bothered Mary.

That's when she had an idea. She went to a craft store and bought some blocks of soft wood, a knife, and a book on wood-carving. Then she got to work. At first, her carvings were crude and crooked, but with practice she began to improve. She carried the supplies with her in a paper shopping bag, and when she found herself sitting and waiting, she took out her wood and began to whittle. Because the wood chips fell into the shopping bag, she had no mess to clean up. Though she often attracted stares when she whittled in waiting rooms, she found that most people were really fascinated by what she was doing. Even better, she found that she could whittle just about anywhere!

Later, when Mary's mother came to live with her, Mary had even less time to get out and be active like she once was, but she found that being able to sit and carve helped fill her time and kept her feeling productive. She also managed to get some time away to attend a woodcarving class at a nearby college. One of her proudest moments was when the instructor showed Mary's carvings to the class and asked if she would be willing to sell him one for his collection.

It wasn't until Mary's caregiving responsibilities forced her to come up with a different kind of hobby that she rediscovered a childhood love—only this time she was the one doing the woodcarvings. Eventually, she was able to finagle some time from her mother to once again take some weekend camping trips with her children and their families or Saturday hikes with her husband. But she continues to carve. Now her children and grandchildren treasure her works.

Is there something you have always wanted to do? You may have more time than you realize to do it. If your hobby is portable like Mary's, you may find it a respite from the anxiety and boredom that can come with having a loved one in the hospital, sitting by a bedside, or waiting for a doctor to deliver test results.

Take Time to Exercise

If you want your life to move in the right direction, it's important that you, well, get moving. I can't say enough about exercise. Regular exercise can strengthen your heart, build strong bones and muscles, increase your energy, improve your mood, boost your metabolism, trim down your body, and even reduce your risk of some cancers. Furthermore, it can give you opportunities to meet people and to set and achieve new goals. And it is economical—you don't have to buy expensive equipment, and many health clubs offer discounts if you join for a year or more. As if all that's not enough, once you give exercise a fair try, you may realize how much *fun* it is. You may get hooked. Deidre is a good—though perhaps extreme—example.

Seeing Deidre now, it's hard to believe that she was once sedentary and overweight. She credits her athletic lifestyle and success as a marathon runner to her father's long illness. "The year my father had his bypass surgery and then spent weeks in the intensive care unit with complications, I became both angry and frustrated. I needed a way to let out my frustrations," she recalls. Deidre often became weary of sitting in the ICU waiting room, yet she didn't want to miss her short but precious permitted visiting time with her father. Driving home between visits was not an option. She lived an hour and a half a way.

One day, a nurse told Deidre about a park located about a half-mile from the hospital, where Deidre could take a walk, feed the ducks, or just find some solitude. Deidre gave it a try. She found long walks through the park gave her time to think and relieved some of the frustration she felt sitting in the hospital. Soon her walks became jogs and her jogs became runs.

"When I ran I would tell myself, *I can't control what happens to my father, but I can control what happens to me. I will be strong, my heart will be strong.*"

Whether you just want to do something you *can* control—or if seeing your ailing parent reminds you that you should be caring for your own health—doing regular exercise can help (but be sure to check with your doctor before starting a new exercise regimen). An exercise habit you form now is one you can (and should) keep for years to come.

When Deidre's father left the hospital and went to stay with Deidre and her family, Deidre used his home health aide's morning visits as her time to run errands and run the hills of her neighborhood. By the time her father moved into an assisted-living center two years later, Deidre was sometimes running twenty miles or more at a time. At forty-six, she was feeling stronger and healthier than she had in her twenties. "I was amazed with myself," she said. "I had always been pretty seden-tary. I wanted to exercise, but never seemed to have the time and I hadn't found an exercise that I really enjoyed."

Last Fall, Deidre did something she wouldn't have dared to dream just five years ago—she ran a marathon. Today, she con-tinues to run. Her next-door neighbor and grown daughter have taken up running, and the three of them often run together. She also still manages her father's care and, often, haunting ques-tions pop up. What will I do when my father has demands that assisted living can't meet? How will we afford round-the-clock nursing care? What if he eventually needs more surgery? "I think over all of those things while I'm running, but I also focus on my own health and the sense of accomplishment I feel after a long run," she says. "I don't know what I would do without this outlet."

Attend a Support Group

If you feel overwhelmed with the seemingly neverending re-sponsibilities of caregiving, you can take some comfort in the fact that you're not alone. There are many other people in the same situation who no doubt share your fears, frustration, and utter exhaustion, yet many of them probably live lives that would encourage and inspire you. How do you meet these peo-ple? Through a support group.

Fifteen years ago, when Anita's husband was suffering com-plications from years of diabetes, she joined a support group for caregivers. Each Tuesday morning, she looked forward to the one-and-a-half hour break from her caregiving duties when she would be able to meet with other women and men caring for spouses, parents, and other relatives. Though most of the group discussions focused on the serious challenges of caregiving, Anita was impressed that so many of the long-standing members remained joyful and lighthearted despite their arduous caregiving duties.

She often found herself lingering after a meeting ended to chat with the other members. Occasionally, she stopped for coffee or lunch before returning to her husband. Throughout the week, if she needed a recommendation of a home health aide to help out when the regular one called in sick, an idea for a sugar-free dessert, or a just a sympathetic ear, she knew who to call. Her support group members soon became some of her closest friends and greatest sources of emotional and practical support.

Though Anita's husband died eleven years ago and Anita left the group the following year, the relationships she developed with her fellow members remain strong. In fact, she married one of the other group members, a widower who was caring for both his wife and aging father when he attended the group. Anita and her new husband have just celebrated their sixth anniversary.

If you'd like to attend a support group, check with caregiving organizations and disease-specific nonprofit organizations in your area to see if they offer a group. If you find a group that meets at a time you can attend, visit a few times and take mental notes: Do you like the people in the group? Do they make you feel welcome? Do you have things in common with them? Are they generally upbeat or are they there for a big pity party? Do they seem to have lives outside of caregiving?

While you want a group that will talk about the task at hand—coping with caregiving—you don't want a group that's all gloom and doom. You want to leave the group feeling understood, hopeful, and encouraged—not more hopeless than when you arrived.

Though most people won't meet a future spouse in a support group (and surely shouldn't attend one for that reason), many do gain the resources needed to make it through caregiving and beyond. Some develop deep, long-term friendships with people who understand what they are going through or have been through it themselves in the past. As far as I'm concerned, nothing is more life-giving than having someone you care about who understands and cares about you. To find a support group, check with assisted-living centers, local chapters of various health foundations and disease-specific associations (such as the Alzheimer's Association) or caregivers' organizations. (For organizations and contact information, see Organizations and Web Sites in Appendix 1 in the Resources section at the back of this book.)

Support groups may meet weekly, biweekly, or monthly. Some meet during business hours; others meet in the evenings. Some are even held on the telephone or Internet for people who simply can't get away from their loved one for an hour or two. There is something for everyone.

Reach Out to Others in Need

Okay, I know this sounds crazy. You spend your whole life caring for your sick or aging loved one. How can you possibly do any more for anyone else? Why would you even *want* to?

Here's the answer: Because I am convinced that the more you do for others—as long as you don't neglect yourself—the more you get in return. Helping others takes the focus off your own problems and puts them in perspective. Perhaps your own situation isn't as bad as what others must face.

I have known many women who have benefited from look-ing beyond their own situations when faced with adversity. For example, one woman whose husband suffered a stroke began a support group for spouses of stroke victims. The group was a source of inspiration and comfort for all of the members—most of all, the woman who started it.

Another woman, when she had trouble finding people to oc-casionally sit for her aging mother, began a sitting co-op. Call-ing on friends and friends of friends, she got the names of about twenty women in her area who were willing to take turns help-ing one another. In the few years since the co-op started, several of the women participating have become close friends, provid-ing emotional support to one another in addition to the physi-cal hours they contribute.

Another woman I know takes off one evening a month to prepare and serve dinner at a homeless shelter. "Sometimes, when I start feeling bad about my own life, I go to the shelter and I realize how much I have to be grateful for," she told me. "Sure, I get weary caring for my dad, but at least I have a roof over my head, clean clothes to wear, nutritious meals to eat, and medical care when I need it—a lot more than the people who come to the shelter."

When you get bogged down in your daily care duties, step-ping outside your own world to care in a different way can give you a greater sense of purpose and can help you see your place in the universe. When life isn't going the way we want it to, it's easy to focus on what we don't have, but it's much more pro-ductive to focus on what we *do* have.

A word of caution: Don't stress yourself by taking on too many outside activities. Try to find a helpful activity you can do on an occasional basis. You don't want another commitment that's going to overstress you or take too much time away from the people in your life who need you. If you find a worthwhile project that is rewarding, you can always decide to devote more time to it once your family caregiving responsibilities have eased or ended.

Don't Forget the Rest of the Famly

One of the most common laments I hear from caregivers is that in committing themselves to the care of one family member, they neglect their relationships with the others.

Such was the case with Carla. She was just twenty-eight when she married Steve, who was forty. Because Steve was an only child and his widowed mother was already in early her seventies when they married, Carla was pretty certain that she would one day be caring for her mother-in-law. Sure enough, ten years into their marriage, Steve's mother broke a hip and moved in with Carla, Steve, and their two young children. Caring for Steve's mother and her own children took all of Carla's time and energy.

"While I was constantly caring for and doing for my mother-in-law, I rarely saw my own mother who lived across town," Carla recalled sadly. "Because my mother-in-law was older and in ill health, I devoted myself to caring for her. I thought there would always be time later for my mother, who was just sixty and in apparently great health."

That plan ended one day, however, when Carla got a call from her younger sister, saying that their mother had suffered a heart attack that morning. Three days later, Carla's mother died in the hospital. Her mother-in-law, on the other hand, lived thirteen more years to the age of ninety-five!

By focusing almost exclusively on the care of her mother-in-law, Carla neglected a relationship that had been a source of comfort and happiness for her throughout her life—the relationship with her own mother. She missed out on the happiness she and her mother could have shared those years and the pleasure of including her own mother in her family's activities.

"Though I don't regret caring for my mother-in-law, I do regret making her care the exclusive focus of our family life," Carla told me. "The time I missed with my own mother can never be made up now."

Other women have told me similar stories. Often these stories involve their husbands or children. Several women have told me they were so busy caring for their aging parents that they didn't realize—until too late—how much their marriages had suffered. Another woman told me that she assumed her thirteen-year-old son was in school and doing fine until one day she got a visit from a police officer. For several days during the previous few weeks, her son had ridden his bicycle to the park instead of to school, she learned. The day of the officer's visit, the boy had been caught breaking into a parked car to steal a video game and some CDs.

Now wait—this isn't supposed to be a guilt trip. I'm *not* saying that your loved ones will die, betray you, or get into trouble with the law if you focus on your job as caregiver. Nor am I saying that if any of these things do happen that it's your fault. What I *am* saying is that life is short—sometimes shorter than we expect—and relationships can be fragile unless we work to make them stronger. If possible, take at least a few minutes of each day to *show* love to everyone you love.

Nurture your relationships and work to fix other problems in your life. Good communication with all of your family members—not just your aging parent—is essential. I am convinced that some women throw themselves into caregiving as a way to avoid a bigger problem of a failing marriage or troubled children. Problems don't often go away on their own—they only get bigger. Address them before they escalate. If you expect to reap the benefits of a good life later on—well-behaved, responsible kids, and a well-behaved, responsible husband, for example— you need to remember to put some effort into these relationships *now*.

Maintain Friendships

Whether you anticipate becoming a caregiver, are consumed with caregiving, or are wondering what to do now that your caregiving tasks have ended, you need the support of good friends. Unfortunately, many women put friendships on the back burner while contending with the more immediate demands of an aging parent or spouse.

Ruth knows that all too well. Before she finally admitted that she could no longer care for her ill husband alone, Ruth scarcely left his side. "I promised to stick by him for better for worse, in sickness and health, forsaking all others," says Ruth. "The years following his stroke were definitely the worst of my life, but I stuck with him. Unfortunately, forsaking all others meant giving up friendships that could have helped me through that difficult time."

After her husband's stroke, Ruth stopped going out with her group of friends. She gave up her bridge club and her position as secretary in her women's club. When friends called, it seemed she was always too busy tending to her husband to talk. After a while, her friends stopped calling. By the time her husband moved into a nursing home three years later, Ruth was practically a recluse. "I was lonely. I missed Harry and I missed my friends. But friends were nowhere around."

It can be difficult to keep up friendships *and* caregiving duties, but if you work at it, friendships can last and even grow stronger.

In fact, it's often during difficult times that you learn who your true friends are. Sue learned that lesson when her mother broke her hip and came to stay with Sue's family during her recovery.

Sue was active and outgoing and had lots of friends. At first, Sue's friends, neighbors, and coworkers expressed their concern over Sue's mother and offered to help. "If there's anything I can do for you, just call," they would say. Sue tested the depths of their sincerity one afternoon while waiting for her mother to complete an outpatient procedure. Sitting in the hospital waiting room, she received a call on her cell phone from her son's school. During a ball game in P.E., he was hit by a foul ball. Aside from having broken glasses and a bruise, the school nurse thought he was okay, but suggested that Sue take him to see his doctor just in case.

Because her husband was out of town for the week, Sue immediately thought of those who had offered their help. She quickly began calls to her friends to ask if one might come wait for her mother while she tended to her son. She made twelve calls and received an equal number of "sorry, but I . . ." before she reached her neighbor Samantha who said, "I can be there in ten minutes." Needless to say, Sue will always remember Samantha as a true friend.

I'm not saying that friends have to be at your beck and call. But anyone can say the words, "If there's anything I can do to help . . ." Good friends are willing to make sacrifices in order to follow through. Of course, that goes both ways. Being a friend takes some sacrifice and work on your part, as well. When friends call, do your best to speak for a minute or ask when you might call them back—and again, *follow through*. Though your caregiving duties may prevent you from running to your friends' rescue when they need help, think of other ways you might help them or make simple gestures to let them know you care. Cards on special occasions, notes, or e-mails will let your friends know you're thinking of them.

If you think you don't have the time or energy to maintain friendships, think again. Good friends are flexible. With a little creativity, you can enjoy your friends while doing the things you must do anyway.

One time, a friend and I—both pressed for time—shopped for groceries together. We enjoyed walking the store aisles and comparing grocery lists, and when our visit was over, our shopping was done as well. Another time, I met a friend for lunch while her son was in the dentist office three stories above the restaurant getting braces. We had just as much fun visiting and chatting under those circumstances as we would have if we had planned a more elaborate lunch date.

You can also try taking friends on errands—to the dry cleaners, to the post office, or to the baby store to purchase a shower gift, for example. If nothing else, you both get your errands done and enjoy the time you spend together in the car, talking and listening to music.

If your friend lives or works near the office where your mom has a doctor's appointment, see if you can stop by and see her or meet her for coffee—or, better yet, ask if she might sit with you in the waiting room while you wait for your parent. This will not only be a good opportunity for the two of you to get together, it will probably make your parent happy too. Your parent will probably feel less guilty having you wait for her if she knows you're visiting with a friend.

Keep *Your* Medical Appointments

When you're a caregiver, time is a precious commodity. It's hard to handle all your commitments and still manage time for yourself. But doing so is essential. Many working women I know tell me they spend so much time taking their parents to medical appointments that they have no sick or personal leave left for themselves. Others say they grow so weary of taking their parents to doctors that they can't muster the energy to make appointments to see their own doctors.

If you spend a lot of time in medical offices with your parents, probably the last thing you want to do when you have a break is to go to another one. But you must. I tell women that even if they have to pay someone to take their parents to appointments, they must not neglect their own health checkups. You must take time to tend to your own health—particularly if you plan to have a life after caregiving.

Despite the daily reminder of the problems that poor health can cause, many caregivers seem to believe they are invincible. I can't count the number of times I have heard women say, "I don't get sick. I don't have *time* to get sick."

Though you may be relatively young yourself, don't assume that your youth ensures good health. Regardless of your age, you should have regular physical exams, including screening tests for several types of cancer. The American Cancer Society (www.cancer.org) recommends the following screening tests for women:

Breast cancer

Ages twenty to thirty-nine: clinical breast exam every three years. Age forty and older: mammogram and clinical breast exam yearly.

Cervical cancer

Three years after beginning vaginal intercourse (no later than age twenty-one): pap smear and exam yearly.

Endometrial cancer

For women at increased risk: Discuss the possibility of yearly exams and the advisability of endrometrial biopsies with your doctor.

Colon and rectal cancer

Age fifty and older: fecal occult blood test, double contrast barium enema, and/or flexible sigmoidoscopy every five years; colonoscopy every ten years (If you have a family history of colon cancer, speak with your doctor about the possible need for earlier or more frequent tests.)

Source: ACS Cancer Detection Guidelines, 2004

Depending on your age and other risk factors (including family history of heart disease, certain cancers, and other health problems), your doctor may recommend other exams as well.

As we discussed earlier in the book, the stress of caregiving can increase your risk of a number of different health problems. In fact, one study shows that 25 percent of women caregivers have health problems as a result of their caregiving activities. Fortunately, virtually every health problem is more treatable when you catch it early and keep up with your treatment.

If you find that you simply can't make more trips to medical offices, look for ways to double up. If your mother needs to see her cardiologist, for example, see if there isn't a suitable eye doctor in the building so you could have a checkup at the same time. If your mother needs to see the dentist, schedule your dental appointment for that day as well. A big plus to this: If she finishes first, she can wait for you, and you have a built-in sitter with the person at the front desk of her doctor's office. While obviously there are some medical specialists you won't want to—or shouldn't—change or share, sometimes changing providers makes health care for both of you more convenient.

Neglecting your health now will not only make it more difficult to perform your caregiving tasks, it will also leave you open to health problems that will affect your ability to engage in activities you love. And remember, odds are you won't be a caregiver forever. You don't want to be saddled with your own illnesses when your caregiving job has ended.

Eat Well

Though it may be easy to grab a burger between nursing home visits, drown your frustration in a quart of chocolate ice cream, or relieve your fatigue with a giant cola or extra cup of coffee, you'd be a lot better off sticking to a healthy diet. Just like exercise and regular doctor visits, a proper diet is essential to your good health and wellness—both now, as you care for your loved one, and later, when you'll want many years of good health left to enjoy your independence.

It's no secret that eating right will not only help you feel better, it can also help you look better. When my friend Janet's mother was undergoing cancer treatment, I noticed Janet was putting on a significant amount of weight. One day she told me she was tired of the way she looked, but she was simply too busy and stressed with her job and her mom's illness to commit to a strict diet.

If you think you're too busy or too stressed to start a diet, think again. Eating healthfully doesn't have to mean following a strict low-calorie diet or restricting yourself to foods purchased from a weight-loss chain. In fact, you'd be better off to make some long-term changes to your existing diet and lifestyle. When you're hungry and in a hurry, have a piece of fruit instead of a candy bar, for example. Or have a glass of water with your fast-food salad instead of a thick shake with a burger.

Now more than ever you need to take care of yourself—so you can take care of your parent. While you can't completely control your medical destiny, you can reduce your risk of many health problems by eating nutritiously. Caring for a person who is aging and ill should be a reminder of what a blessing good health is. Eating well will help increase the odds that you'll be in good health and enjoy your life for years to come.

Fix Yourself Up

If you stay home caring for a loved one, it's easy to roll out of bed and put on the most convenient and comfortable thing you have—be it sweats or a fuzzy, warm robe—and then keep it on all day. But try and force yourself to get dressed—at least most days.

Whether you have somewhere to go or not, just getting dressed gives you the sense that there's work to be done, fun to be had, opportunities waiting. If those opportunities arise—even if it's just answering the door to sign for a FedEx package—you'll be dressed and ready. Expect the unexpected!

I'm not suggesting you overdo it or be impractical. You don't need to wear your best business suit to drive your mother to the doctor. Nor do you need to put on a slinky cocktail dress and stiletto heels to pick up prescriptions and prepare her lunch. But

I am convinced that people act according to the way they dress. Wear your comfy sweats and you're more likely to lie on the couch and let life pass you by than if you wear something you'd feel good about going out in—a favorite sundress, a pair of crisp slacks with a knit top, or jeans with a pretty sweater. The same goes for applying makeup and doing your hair. Keep it simple, but don't let it slide completely. Your husband will appreciate the little extra effort too!

Some older people—particularly ones with dementia—lose interest in grooming, bathing, or changing their clothes. That doesn't mean their caregiver has to also. If you dress nicely and bathe each day, you're also setting a good example for your parent.

Caregiving shouldn't be all drudgery. If your mother is able, take her clothes shopping or make an appointment for the two of you to have manicures or have your hair done. A day out and a new look can be a morale booster for both of you.

Count Your Blessings

Regardless of how many things go wrong or how hard we must struggle for our successes, most of us in this country are blessed. I know it sounds simplistic, but sometimes all it takes to get a new lease on life is to count your blessings. Spend some time making a mental list (or perhaps even a written one) of all you have to be grateful for—a warm home, a loving family, plentiful food, good health, and a dependable job. (Don't forget the less obvious, such as the seventh-grade teacher who sparked your interest in history or the automobile accident you averted while driving to the mall.)

On the list, also remember to include the things you like about you. For example, "I am grateful to be hardworking and honest. I am grateful for my artistic talent, my ability to cheer up friends, my flair for Cajun cooking."

I have found that people with interesting, fulfilling lives also have a healthy, realistic sense of themselves. They don't feel inferior; nor do they have grandiose ideas that they are somehow superior to others or that they must excel at everything they try. They accept who they are, change what they can, and make a life for themselves. These are also the kind of people who focus on finding a solution instead of dwelling on the problem.

Think of all you have and all you can do. Then set out to achieve your goals.

Clean Up and Clear Out

Do you have clothes in your closet you haven't worn for years? Shoe boxes full of recipes you clipped, stashed, and never tried? Stacks of magazines you'll never read? Materials for a quilt that you have never sewed? A long list of phone messages that you never returned?

If so, you have a problem that extends beyond a messy house. You have the propensity to cling to and collect clutter that can keep you from living life to the fullest and pursuing your dreams.

When Barbara Sher, author of *How to Live the Life You Love: In Ten Easy Step-by-Step Lessons* (Delacorte Press, 1996), bought a vacation home in the country, she wrote: "There was a nice old barn behind the house full of stuff: gardening things, boxes of books, old furniture, light fixtures, and tools. Parked in the middle of it all was a '61 Chevy, which the previous owners had always planned to restore."

Every summer, Sher would go to the country on the weekends and spend Saturday trying to organize the contents of the barn, deciding what to keep, what to give away, what to toss, and what to restore. Every Sunday she would return to the city exhausted and frustrated. Although the contents of the barn held endless possibilities, they were also keeping her from enjoying her weekend getaways.

And then one day, while she was at home in the city, the barn burned to the ground. "My first feeling was one of utter dismay," she wrote. "What a waste. I was stricken, ready to cry. My second feeling was enormous relief."

Whether in the form of unread magazines, unworn clothes, undone projects, or barns (or merely drawers) full of stuff to sort through, the clutter in our lives keeps us from facing the important stuff. "Clutter in the background gives the illusion that you're surrounded by projects just waiting to be done," says Sher. "It makes you feel that life is full of potential. The things that crowd the corners and shelves may look like junk to other people, but to you every single item represents an opportunity."

As long as there are projects to be done and clutter to be sorted through, it's hard to make a commitment to something bigger. But as Sher found when the barn burned, permanently eliminating clutter can be liberating.

❧ *10 Tips to Clean Up or Cope with Clutter* ❧

To cope with and/or eliminate the clutter in your life, consider why you are keeping it and what more enjoyable activities you could be doing to fill your time once it's gone. The answer may be much more exciting than a life of sorting through or stepping over your stuff. Ready to take a chance and get rid of some of the stuff that's crowding your life? Try these tips, some of which Barbara Sher recommends, to help rid your home and life of clutter.

1. *Set a date.* Give yourself a deadline for completing unfinished projects (old socks that need mending, coupons that need sorting, a chair that needs refinishing) and stick to it. If the date arrives and you still haven't done the project—or at least made progress toward it—toss the project or pass it along to a friend.

2. *Help someone.* Think of someone who can put your old clothing, stacks of books, and excess kitchen items to good use. You'll not only get rid of clutter, you may also get a tax deduction.

3. *Have a yard sale.* Place your ad, make signs, mark your items, and then place them in the yard and wait. Call a charity to pick up what you don't sell.

4. *Toss ten things.* Begin a campaign to throw out ten things from every room as often as you think of it. Stick with it and, in a week or two, you'll start to see a difference.

5. *Issue ultimatums.* If your home is filled with stuff your grown kids or other relatives left behind, let them know you are cleaning up and give them an ultimatum to pick up their stuff by a certain date or you'll get rid of it.

6. *Get some help.* Sometimes it helps to have an objective friend step in and help you dispose of your clutter. Put on some music, order pizza or Chinese food, and make it a mini-party.

7. *Schedule an appointment.* You somehow manage to keep your other appointments. Schedule an appointment with yourself to clean one room in your house or finish one project—or block off three hours one afternoon each week. Mark the time and date on your calendar and then do it!

8. *Take one room at a time.* Clear out the clutter in the smallest and least cluttered room of your house and then, each week, tackle a new room. If you end up with one room with all the clutter from the others, shut the door—tightly—and walk away.

9. *Hire professionals.* A professional estate sale planner (a person who helps families identify and sell off items of value from a deceased loved one's estate) may be willing to go through your house, help clean it out, sell anything of value—even if it's just excessive Tupperware® or coffee mugs crowding your kitchen cabinets—and give you a percentage of the proceeds.

10. *Let it be.* Admit that your big box of photos may never be glued neatly in a photo album and the artwork your eight-year-old has done since kindergarten may never be framed and hung. Some things aren't worth stressing over—let them be.

When your days are filled with caregiving tasks and concerns, it's not always easy to get your life back. But it's possible—and essential. Remember to live your life, as your parent's condition is not contingent on your constant fretting and presence. Be a part of the present; live in it and enjoy it. Most of all, don't let life or time pass you by!

CONCLUSION

Caring for an aging parent is one of the hardest jobs you will ever have. There will most likely be times when you'll feel that you just can't go on—times when it seems you and your family can't agree on anything; times when no one, including your parent, appreciates what you're doing, yet everyone makes you feel *invisible*; times when you feel you just can't pick up another prescription, schedule another appointment, lose another night's sleep, or see your parent slip further away from the strong, competent adult who once cared for and protected you. Yes, there will be times when every day, indeed every hour, feels like a struggle for survival.

It's times like those that you must reach out for help. You *must*. If nothing else, I hope this book has shown you the importance of not going it alone and has given you some useful, concrete advice for starting to get the help you need *now*.

Though it may seem hard to believe at this point in your life, your caregiving duties won't go on forever. When your days as a caregiver have ended, you'll want to look back and know you did the best you could for your parent with all of the resources available to you. You'll want to know you made the most of the last days, months, and years with your loved one—surviving the bad times but always remembering to seek out and cherish the good.

Just as important, you'll want to have a life to return to— filled with people you love, activities that interest you, and the good health to enjoy them. Your parent would want nothing less for you.

Appendix 1

HELP AND RESOURCES FOR CAREGIVERS

Many resources are available for caregivers. For help with under-standing eldercare options, finding support groups, or learning more about your parent's medical conditions, check out this section.

ORGANIZATIONS AND WEB SITES

The following organizations and Web sites offer information and resources to help caregivers.

The Family Caregiver Alliance
(415) 434-3388
www.caregiver.org

National Family Caregivers Association
(800) 896-3650
www.nfcacares.org

Administration on Aging
(202) 619-7501
www.aoa.gov

PUBLICATIONS

The following publications provide useful and, in some cases, inspirational information for caregivers.

Today's Caregiver Magazine
(800) 829-2734
www.caregiver.com

Caregiving Newsletter
(773) 334-5794
www.caregiving.com

REFERRAL SERVICES AND WEB SITES

The following sites can help you locate housing, professionals, and other help for your loved one.

A Place for Mom
This free referral service helps families find nursing homes, assisted-living centers, and home care.
(866) 666-3239 (MOM-DAD9)
www.aplaceformom.com

National Association of Professional Geriatric Care Managers
This organization and its Web site offer referrals to geriatric care managers in your geographic area.
(520) 881-8008
www.caremanager.org

Find Senior Housing
Check out this site for general information on housing options for seniors and referrals to specific services by geographic area.
www.seniorhousing.net

Eldercare Locator
On this government site, you'll find information on local services, based on your zip code.
(800) 677-1116
www.eldercare.gov

National Directory of U.S. Home Care and Health Care Service Providers
Use this site to find a home care or home health care service provider near you. It also features general information on caregiving and services and options that are available.
www.seniormag.com

HELP FOR SENIOR HEALTH PROBLEMS

The following organizations offer information and resources for people with health problems common in older adults. For general information on seniors' health problems, log on to the National Institute on Aging's Web site, *www.nia.nih.gov*. For disease-specific information, check out the following:

Alzheimer's Disease or Memory Loss

Alzheimer's Association
(800) 272-3900
www.alz.org

American Brain Tumor Association
(800) 886-2282
www.abta.org

Arthritis

The Arthritis Foundation
(800) 283-7800
www.arthritis.org

National Institute of Arthritis and Musculoskeletal and Skin Diseases
(877) 226-4267
www.niams.nih.gov

Cancer

American Cancer Society
(800) ACS-2345 (227-2345)
www.cancer.org

National Cancer Institute
(800) 4-CANCER (422-6237)
www.nci.nih.gov

Cardiovascular (Heart) Disease

American Heart Association
(800) AHA-USA-1 (242-8721)
www.americanheart.org

American Stroke Association
(888) 4-STROKE (478-7653)
www.strokeassociation.org

National Heart, Blood and Lung Institute
(301) 592-8573
www.nhlbi.nih.gov

Diabetes

American Diabetes Association
(800) DIABETES (342-2383)
www.diabetes.org

National Institute of Diabetes and Digestive and Kidney Diseases
www.niddk.nih.gov

Hearing Loss

National Institute on Deafness and Other Communication Disorders
National Institutes of Health
(800) 241-1044
(800) 241-1055 (TTY)
www.nidcd.nih.gov

SHHH (Self-Help for Hard of Hearing People)
(301) 657-2248
(301) 657-2249 (TTY)
www.hearingloss.org

Incontinence

National Association for Continence
(800) 252-3337
www.nafc.org

Lung Disease

American Lung Association
(212) 315-8700
www.lungusa.org

National Heart, Lung and Blood Institute
(301) 592-8573
www.nhlbi.nih.gov

Macular Degeneration

Macular Degeneration Foundation
(888) 633-3937
www.eyesight.org

American Macular Degeneration Foundation
(413) 268-7660
www.macular.org

Osteoporosis

National Osteoporosis Foundation
(202) 223-2226
www.nof.org

Appendix 2

RESOURCES FOR SENIORS

BOOKS

Many libraries and major bookstores either carry large-print books or can order them for you upon request. You can also order a wide variety of large-print publications from online booksellers.

Large Print Books
Offers large-print books and magazines, as well as books on audiotape and in foreign languages. A wide selection of novels, cookbooks, biographies, Westerns, mysteries, crosswords, health, science, adventure, romance, history, sewing, sci-fi, fantasy, and more.
www.largeprintbooks.com

Tomfolio
Locate and buy large-print books and other used, collectible, and rare books on this site, which is owned by independent book dealers who guarantee their books.
www.tomfolio.com

Huge Print Press
Is large print not large enough? Huge Print books feature extra-large type. You choose the size type you need.
(877) 527-4377
www.hugeprint.com

Blindreaders Info
Features large-print books and magazines, including *Reader's Digest* and *New York Times Weekly*. You'll also find links to other resources for the visually impaired.
www.blindreaders.info

National Library Service for the Blind and Physically Handicapped (NLS)
Through a national network of cooperating libraries, NLS administers a free library program of Braille and audio materials circulated to eligible borrowers in the United States by postage-free mail.
(800) 424-8567
www.loc.gov/nls

Doubleday Large Print Book Club
(717) 918-4120
www.doubledaylargeprint.com

Barnes and Noble
www.barnesandnoble.com

Amazon.com
www.amazon.com

HOBBIES AND LEISURE PRODUCTS

Hobbies can make your parent's years more enjoyable and fulfilling, occupy otherwise lonely hours, and help take the focus off of *you*. Following are sources of information and products for some of the more popular hobbies among seniors.

Bird watching

Here you'll find free bird clip art, international birding sites, bird calls, and more.
www.seniorliving.about.com

Model trains, card games, and more

You'll find lots of featured links to sites on popular hobbies for seniors.
www.senioryears.com/hobbies.html

Crafts, gardening, gourmet cooking, and dining

If cooking or crafting is your parent's thing, check out this site.
www.zelgo.com/hobbies-seniors.htm

Needlework

Offers free project instructions, patterns, links to craft sites, and more.
www.craftown.com

Other hobby items for seniors

A virtual treasure trove of attractive hobby products and gifts for seniors.
(877) 648-8400
www.goldviolin.com

Games

Shop for large-piece jigsaw puzzles, large-print playing cards, crossword puzzles, and word-search books, card shufflers, and more on this site.
www.seniorstore.com

Music and videos

Classic TV—*I Love Lucy, Burns and Allen, Milton Berle, Jack Benny,* and more—and exercise videos, anniversary, and/or birthday videos
www.seniorstore.com

Crosley record player

Plays all of your parent's old 45 and 33⅓ RPMs. Features state-of-the-art engineering with classic wood cabinet (oak or cherry finish).
(800) 762-1005
www.restorationhardware.com

Gardening tools

You'll find a selection of gardening tools to suit your parent's physical capabilities at the following sites:

Peta (Parent company is located in the United Kingdom, but has a U.S. branch that will ship within the 50 states)
(800) 227-0877
www.peta-uk.com/peta_usa.htm

Gardenscape Ltd.
(888) 472-3266
www.gardenscape.on.ca

SHOPPING

Catalog and online shopping is popular among seniors because it doesn't require finding a parking place, fighting crowds, or spending hours on their feet at the mall. For a good source of products that can help seniors live more comfortably and independently, check out the following online (and offline) catalogs:

Comfort House
(800) 359-7701
www.comforthouse.com

Disability Products
(800) 688-4576
www.disabilityproducts.com

Elder Corner
(888) 777-1816
www.eldercorner.com

Gold Violin
(877) 648-8400
www.goldviolin.com

Home Trends
(800) 810-2340
www.hometrendscatalog.com

Improvements Catalog
(800) 642-2112
www.improvementscatalog.com

Independent Living Aids
(800) 537-2118
www.independentliving.com

Organize Everything
(800) 600-9817
www.organize-everything.com

Solutions Catalog
(877) 718-7901
www.solutionscatalog.com

Senior Shops
(800) 894-9549
www.seniorshops.com

Wired Seniors
www.wiredseniors.com

COMPUTERS AND CYBERSPACE

A computer with Internet access can connect even a homebound elder with the outside world for health and leisure information, family communication, online shopping, and more. The following products and sites may be useful for older adults who use computers.

Adaptive Computer Technology
This site is a guide to sources of information in alternative formats, including electronic text and Web audio, accessible by people with visual and physical handicaps.
www.blindreaders.info

Voice-activated Software
Check local computer stores or the Internet for programs that allow hands-free typing (your parent speaks and the computer does the rest). This technology still has some room for improvement but is certainly a good start. A couple of examples:

Tuscan software
Download from Web site for a free fifteen-day trial.
www.tuscan-software.com

Dragon NaturallySpeaking 7
(800) 245-2133
www.voicerecognition.com

Search engine for the over-50 crowd
Search for virtually anything of interest to seniors.
www.seniorssearch.com

Senior Globe
This Internet Service Provider (ISP) caters to and offers special rates for seniors.
(866) 495-9385
www.seniorglobe.com

Senior Net
This is a nonprofit organization that dedicates itself to teaching mature adults how to use the computer. They set up classes in local cities and community centers.
(415) 495-4990
www.seniornet.org

ELECTRONICS

Many companies carry products such as large-button telephones and television remote controls, voice-recognition telephones, talking watches and clocks for people with low vision, etc.

Harris Communications
(800) 825-6758
www.harriscomm.com

Hearing Planet
(800) HEAR-NOW (432-7669)
www.hearingplanet.com

Arizona Hearing Online Corp.
(866) 674-3549
www.azhearing.com

Independent Living Aids
(800) 537-2118
www.independentliving.com

SPORTS, FITNESS, AND EXERCISE FOR SENIORS

It's not too late to get in shape or stay fit. Regular physical activity will help your parent (and you) feel better physically and mentally. *(Note: Seniors should speak with their doctors before beginning any type of exercise program.)*

Information

For information on exercise safety tips and exercise for seniors (including illustrations and instructions for sample exercises), contact the following organizations:

American Academy of Orthopaedic Surgeons
(800) 346-2267
www.aaos.org

The American Physical Therapy Association (APTA)
Offers a free booklet titled *Young at Heart: Exercise Tips for Seniors*.
(800) 999-APTA (2782)
www.apta.org/Consumer/ptfordailyliving/youngat

Products

The following are some products, activities, and sources of information you or your aging parent may find helpful.

STATIONARY BICYCLES
As one of the most popular pieces of exercise equipment for young and older people alike, stationary bicycles are relatively inexpensive, fairly safe on fragile joints and bones, and can be adjusted—and readjusted—to your parent's fitness level. Stationary bicycles work the large muscles of the legs to provide a cardiovascular workout. When purchasing an exercise bike, look for one with a sturdy seat. This is particularly important if your parent has balance problems. If your parent has difficulty sitting high, or if a traditional cycle is uncomfortable on the knees or back, you may want to have him or her try a recumbent bike. You can buy stationary bicycles at most sporting goods stores. (www.lifefitness.com).

TREADMILLS
If your parent enjoys walking but busy streets or cold, rainy weather make it difficult to keep up a walking routine, you may want to try a motorized treadmill. Like stationary cycles, treadmills work the legs to provide a cardiovascular workout and can be adjusted to your parent's fitness level. Most can be folded and slid under a bed, which

makes them a nice option for older people living in small apartments. To get a good treadmill, be prepared to spend some money. A smooth operating, motorized model can cost $3,000 or more. Treadmills are available at most sporting goods stores. (www.nordictrack.com).

AQUATIC EXERCISE
Aquatic exercise is one of the safest and gentlest forms of exercise for seniors, offering a good cardiovascular, strengthening, and range-of-motion workout with minimal stress to the bones and joints. And your parent doesn't even have to know how to swim. Most Arthritis Foundation chapters offer aquatic exercise programs. To locate a chapter near you, call (800) 283-7800 or log on to www.arthritis.org. Though no particular equipment is needed for these classes, your parent may want a good pair of aqua shoes to protect his or her feet from the rough pool bottom. Other water exercise products, available through many sporting goods stores, include waterproof radios, webbed gloves, and flotation belts. A selection of water exercise products can also be purchased online at www.waterworkout.com.

POOLS
A popular form of exercise for seniors, swimming works the whole body for a good cardiovascular, strengthening, and range-of-motion workout. If your parent wants his or her own pool but doesn't have the space to put one, check out Endless Pools. With a smooth, adjustable current, endless pools provide the benefits of a full-size pool in a space of just 8 by 14 feet, meaning your parent can have a pool in the garden, basement, or garage. To learn more about Endless Pools, call (800) 233-0741 for a free video or log on to www.endlesspools.com.

STRENGTH-TRAINING EQUIPMENT
Strength training can help aid your parent (and all of us) in combating the age-related declines in muscle mass, bone density, and metabolism. It may also help ease back pain and joint pain and play a role in the management of diabetes. A wide range of strength-training equipment is available, from expensive weight machines to inexpensive "rubber bands." You'll find a selection at most sporting goods stores by calling (866) 283-4242 or online at www.simplefitnesssolutions.com.

GOLF EQUIPMENT
Golf offers a low-impact, range-of-motion workout with plenty of pretty scenery and fresh air. No special equipment is necessary for seniors. Golf clubs and accessories are available at most sporting goods stores and specialized golf shops. To order golf clubs and other items online, check out the following:

Golf Smith
(800) 456-3344
www.golfsmith.com

Roger Dunn Golf Shops
(888) 216-5252
www.rdgolf.com

Serendipity Golf-N-Stuff
(330) 847-0333
www.serendipitygolf-n-stuff.com

Teed Off Golf
(888) 829-4643
www.teedoffgolf.com

Eagle USA Golf Clubs and Accessories Proshop
(714) 556-4161
www.eagleusagolf.com

EXERCISE CLASSES
Many senior centers and YMCAs offer fitness classes for seniors, ranging from tai chi to seated aerobics. Call your local center or YMCA to find out about class offerings or visit YMCA on the Web at www.YMCA.net.

CLOTHING

The effects of arthritis, osteoporosis, strokes, and other health problems can affect your parent's appearance and ability to get dressed. Following are some sources of fashionable yet easy-to-wear clothing for seniors.

Senior Citizens' Shopping
This is an online store especially for older adults, featuring good-looking clothing designed for ease of dressing. The site features fashions for those with arthritis, Alzheimer's, scoliosis, and incontinence problems.
www.modernsenior.net

Buck & Buck Designs
This site carries a large selection of attractive clothing for people with an illness or condition that makes dressing difficult. It features clothing for men and women as well as footwear and accessories.
(800) 458-0600
www.buckandbuck.com

Comfort Clothing
Check them out for apparel adapted to best solve the particular dressing problems of wheelchair users, the elderly, and those suffering from such disabilities as stroke, arthritis, paralysis, diabetes, Alzheimer's disease, edema, and incontinence.
(888) 640-0814
www.comfortclothing.com

Fashion First Online Catalog
They bill themselves as the "Home of adaptable apparel, easy-on easy-off apparel, and nursing home clothing."
(847) 677-7413
www.fashfirst.com

Forde's Functional Fashions
The site offers easy-to-use fashions for people with disabilities and their caregivers.
(800) 531-7705
www.fordes.com

Wardrobe Wagon
This site offers clothing for people with special needs. Free alterations are available.
(800) 992-2737
www.wardrobewagon.com

ONLINE CHAT AND SUPPORT GROUPS

If your parent finds it difficult to get out to make and maintain friendships and social ties, online support groups can provide companionship and a place to vent.

Wired Seniors
Jump right in and start a discussion on any topic you like—government, politics, the weather, health concerns, or Social Security. In no time at all you will have a lively, healthy discussion going with seniors from around the world.
www.wiredseniors.com

Help Guide
For Internet support groups on subjects including bereavement, Alzheimer's, and cancer, log on to this site.
www.helpguide.org

WidowNet
For an online chat group for widows and widowers, check out this site.
www.fortnet.org/WidowNet

How to Care
For online support groups on subjects including hip replacement, caregiving, and dementia, visit this site.
www.howtocare.com

DATING WEB SITES

You don't have to be in your twenties or thirties to look for love on the Web. Several online dating services specialize in helping seniors meet their match.

Seniors Match
It's billed as "The Only Matching Service Exclusively For The Over 50 Age Group."
www.seniorsmatch.com

Pearz Connections for People
Pearz has special features for seniors and retired singles!
www.pearz-senior-personals.com

Match.com
Match.com estimates it is responsible for arranging hundreds of thousands of relationships for its members, and it has a special section dedicated specifically for seniors.
www.match.com

Third Age Connections
This is a personals Web site for the over forty set. Log on to make real connections and, find romance, companionship, friendship, and more.
www.thirdageconnections.com

Seniors Dating
Log on to this site to meet other seniors online for friendship, chatting, dating, and more. Log on to this site to meet marriage-minded senior men and women.
www.50yearsplus.com

Senior Friend Finder
This is a popular site for people over fifty looking to meet others for romance, dating, and more.
www.seniorfriendfinder.com

DRIVING SAFETY

Aging-related changes in vision, reflexes, and dexterity can make driving more hazardous for seniors. The following can help make your parent safer on the road.

AARP Driver Safety Program

The nation's first and largest classroom driver refresher course specially designed for motorists age fifty and older, this program helps older drivers improve their skills while teaching them to avoid accidents and traffic violations. The site also features a safe-driving quiz, publications, tips, information on car insurance discounts, and further resources.
(888) 227-7669
www.aarp.org/drive

National Highway Transportation Safety Administration

This organization offers information on safety issues, injury prevention, air bags, crash tests, and much more. It also offers a free booklet titled *Driving Safely While Aging Gracefully* that outlines the physical changes associated with aging, as well as tips on coping with them so that older drivers can remain safe drivers.
(888) 327-4236
www.nhtsa.dot.gov

AAA Foundation for Traffic Safety

The AAA Foundation for Traffic Safety publishes *Drivers 55 Plus: Test Your Own Performance,* which provides specific safety suggestions based on the driver's answers to fifteen questions. Your local AAA club or state department of motor vehicles may also be able to suggest a certified driving school offering courses for seniors.
www.aaafoundation.org

Gadgets to Make Driving Easier and Safer

Items such as panoramic rear-view mirrors, lumbar support cushions, travel pillows, and even a "lazy Susan for people" that can help elders get in and out of their cars are available through the following Web sites:

Elder Corner
(888) 777-1816
www.eldercorner.com

Hammacher Schlemmer
(800) 321-1484
www.hammacherschlemmer.com

Products for Seniors
(800) 566-6561
www.productsforseniors.com/automobile

Senior Shops
(800) 894-9549
www.seniorshops.com

Senior-Friendly Car Features

Increasingly, car manufacturers are considering seniors and people with disabilities when designing cars. The result: Features that make driving more pleasant for seniors, middle-agers, and younger adults alike. The following is a list of features to look for when purchasing a new or newer model used car:

Remote keyless entry: Eliminates fumbling in the purse or pocket for keys, having to grip and turn a key to get into the car. A plus: As long as you remember your code, you can't lock yourself out!

Shorter wheel base: A shorter wheel base makes it easier to handle the car and get into and out of parking spaces—a plus for anyone who has difficulty parking, particularly those with stiffness of their arms, shoulders, or upper back or limited range of motion.

Power seats: Seniors (and others) can easily adjust the driver's seat for maximum comfort and visibility. Look for models with a "memory" feature that allow your parent to return the driver's seat back to his or her preferred position if more than one person drives the car.

Cruise control: A popular option in cars for a number of years, cruise control keeps older adults with foot, knee, or hip problems from having to keep a foot on the gas pedal. Some newer versions automatically adjust the speed to maintain a safe distance from the car in front of you.

Adjustable pedals: Using a button on the car's dashboard, drivers can adjust the height of the brake and gas pedals. This feature is especially welcome for drivers with short (or long) legs or those who have knee or hip pain.

Bench seats: Once standard on family cars, front bench seats (and, in some cases, back seats) were replaced by bucket seats in the '80s and '90s. But due to popular demand, they're back on many car models. Many seniors find bench seats more comfortable, easier to get into, and less confining than low-sitting bucket seats.

Leather interior: For older people who find it hard to slide in and out of a car, smooth leather is preferable to velour or other upholstery material that catches, and is more durable than vinyl (which was popular in older model cars).

Seat heaters: Though these are great for anyone who lives in cold climate (particularly if they must park outdoors), heated seats are popular among older drivers, who may have thin skin and poor circulation that make them vulnerable to the cold. Seat heaters are especially welcome to seniors with stiff hip joints or lower back pain.

Tilt steering wheel: This feature can make it easier for your parent to get in and out of the car (tilt it up and out of the way when entering or exiting) as well as make driving more comfortable for seniors with sore backs or shoulders or those who sit low due to osteoporosis of the spine.

SENIOR-FRIENDLY HOTELS

Many hotels offer special accessible rooms and/or discounted rates for seniors. The following lodging chains offer chain-wide discounts for seniors. To find out about the availability of accessible rooms, contact the hotel you are interested in directly. (Note: I have found that the toll-free reservation numbers—that serve all hotels in a chain—can't always provide or have accurate information on individual establishments.)

Choice Hotels (Clarion Hotels, Quality Inns, Sleep Inns, Friendship Inns, Comfort Inn, Comfort Suites, Main Stay Suites, Rodeway Inns, and Econo Lodges)
Hotels in this chain offer 20 to 30 percent discounts to people over age sixty and smaller discounts to people fifty to sixty. (To qualify, you must make reservations through the chain's toll-free number.)
(800) 4-CHOICE (424-6423)
www.choicehotels.com

Days Inns
Most Days Inns give discounts ranging from 15 to 50 percent to members of its September Days Club. Membership is free to anyone over fifty.
(800) 344-3636
www.daysinn.com

Howard Johnson's
All locations offer 15 percent for seniors sixty years and older.
(800) I-GO-HOJO (446-4656)
www.hojo.com

Marriott Hotels (Courtyard by Marriott, Residence Inn, and Fairfield Inn)
Many locations offer discounts ranging from 10 to 50 percent off rooms and 20 percent off food and nonalcoholic beverages to AARP members.
Marriott (800) 228-9290
Courtyard by Marriott (800) 346-4000
Residence Inn (800) 331-3131
Fairfield Inns (800) 322-4000
www.marriott.com

Radisson Hotels
Hotels in this chain offers discounts of 25 to 40 percent off regular rates to people fifty and older.
(800) 333-3333
www.radisson.com

Ramada Inn
Members of "Ramada Best Years" Club receive a 25 percent discount at all locations.
(800) 2-RAMADA (272-6232)
www.ramada.com

Sheraton Hotels
Most Sheratons give a 25 percent discount to people over 65. (Some restrictions apply.)
(800) 325-3535
www.sheraton.com

SENIOR TOUR GROUPS AND TRAVEL WEB INFORMATION

With the responsibilities of childrearing and career behind, many seniors dream of traveling around the world—or, at least, to some nearby towns. Senior-geared travel groups can help make those dreams come true. If your parent has "wanderlust," check out the following:

Travel Information

AARP Trips n' Travel
Members receive discount travel deals.
www.aarp.org/travel

Independent Traveler
Links to discounts on airlines, hotels, cars, trains, buses, elderhostels, and parks. The site also offers a free weekly newsletter.
www.independenttraveler.com

Info Hub Specialty Travel Guide
Search more than 11,000 guided or self-guided specialty vacations offered by more than 1,300 travel suppliers.
www.infohub.com

The Retirement Net
For retirement homes or communities, this site offers a lot of options.
www.retirenet.com

Seniors Site
This site offers tips on tours and travel packages for seniors.
www.seniors-site.com/travel/tours.html

Zelgo
Look here for listings of trips and links to trips and travel information for seniors on the go.
www.zelgo.com (click on Travel)

Senior Travel Agencies and Tours

Elder Hostel
Nonprofit, all-inclusive educational programs for seniors.
(877) 426-8056
www.elderhostel.org

Elder Treks
Adventure travel for seniors to more than fifty different countries.
(800) 741-7956
www.eldertreks.com

Galasam International
Does your parent want to travel to the Galapagos Islands? This agency offers senior tours and cruises.
www.galapagos-seniors.com

Grand Travel
Grandparents and grandkids travel together in this program dedicated to making lasting family memories.
(800) 247-7651
www.grandtrvl.com

Interhostel Learning Vacations
Appeals to various interests and cultures and offers travel around the world.
(800) 733-9753
www.learn.unh.edu/interhostel

Rockport Tours

Trips offered by this agency range from day trips to a Houston Astros game to Alaskan cruises.
(888) 937-3488
www.rockporttours.com

Senior Summer School

Affordable educational opportunities for seniors on campuses throughout the United States and Canada.
(800) 847-2466
www.seniorsummerschool.com

Senior World Tours

This agency offers seniors-only tours designed for active mature adults who are in physically good condition and would like to try something different for a winter vacation. Destinations offered include the Tetons, Yellowstone Park, and Cowboy Village Resort at Togwotee.
(888) 355-1686
www.seniorworldtours.com

Sandersons Scenic Tours

This company specializes in group coach tours, including senior coach tours and seniors' holidays to various destinations in Australia and New Zealand.
www.sandersons.com.au

Red Carpet Tours

Check here for day trips and overnight trips and cruises to a variety of destinations for seniors.
(407) 254-0474
www.mearstours.com

Travel and Learn

"A luxury field trip" offers learning tips on trips to many different countries.
(800) 235-9114
www.travellearn.com

Transportation Benefits and Discounts

Being over fifty-five can earn your parent (and perhaps you) discounts on travel packages, airfares, hotels, and other travel services. Following are some good deals you should know about.

AIRLINES

Due to industry-wide financial problems, most major airlines no longer offer the senior discounts and perks they did pre-9/11. However, seniors traveling on some airlines may get a small discount for both themselves and a companion. Inquire about senior discounts when purchasing tickets. Here are some examples of the types of senior discounts airlines offer:

Continental Airlines

Continental offers senior fares to selected travel destinations for passengers who are sixty-five and older. Ask for more details on these fares when you make your reservation, or when you make your booking online select the seniors (age sixty-five and older) category.
(800) 441-1135 (a dedicated senior hotline)
www.continental.com

Southwest Airlines

Southwest offers special senior fares to travelers sixty-five years of age or older. For details on fares, limitations, and any restrictions, contact a Southwest Airlines reservations sales agent or a travel agent. Fares are subject to change until tickets are purchased, but senior fare tickets are fully refundable.
(800) I-FLY-SWA (435-9792)
www.southwestairlines.com

United Airlines

United's Silver Wings Plus program is a membership program that offers more than just airline discounts.
(800) 720-1765 (a dedicated senior hotline)
www.silverwingsplus.com

BUSES, TRAINS, NATIONAL PARKS, AND MOBILE HOMES
Amtrak
Amtrak offers a 15 percent discount to seniors on all but first-class tickets.
(800) USA-RAIL (872-7245)
www.amtrak.com

Greyhound
The bus line occasionally (not always) offers discount ticket to seniors. Before booking, call to see if they have promotional specials for seniors.
(800) 752-4841
www.greyhound.com

National Parks
The National Park Services offers a $10 "Golden Age Passport" for seniors. The one-time fee will get any senior sixty-two or older into any National Park for life. To get your passport, apply at any National Park entrance or log on to the park service's Web site.
www.nps.gov

Manufactured Homes Marketplace
Information on mobile homes and RV parks in Florida for seniors.
www.mkpmag.com

INDEX

ABOUT THE AUTHOR

Cited as America's leading, impassioned champion for the dignity and independence of those over fifty, Alexis Abramson is an inspiring speaker, caregiving consultant, successful author, and award-winning entrepreneur. Her message of respect for elders, and solutions for barrier-free and independent living in later years, have been featured in many national publications including *TIME*, *Forbes*, and *People* magazines.

Abramson has appeared as an on-air expert gerontologist for NBC's *Today* show since 1997. She also is sought after as a keynote speaker at conferences, bringing awareness of senior and caregiving issues to corporations, consumers, government agencies, and nonprofit groups. As a consultant to industry, she is called upon to help make products senior-friendly, and employees more sensitive to the needs of mature Americans. She has acted on behalf of older Americans before such organizations as the American Association of Retired Persons, the Arthritis Foundation, Duracell, and Century 21, among many others.

In addition to *The Caregiver Survival Handbook*, Abramson is the author of *Home Safety for Seniors*, a room-by-room reference and idea-book for making independent senior and homebound living easier.

Abramson was inducted into Sigma Phi Omega the National Academic Honor and Professional Society in Gerontology, and received the 2000 and 2001 *Working Woman* Magazine General Entrepreneurial Excellence Award as well as the 1998 American Society of Aging Outstanding Small Business Award.